God's Will

Our Dwelling Place

God's Will

Our Dwelling Place

andrew murray

WHITAKER
HOUSE

All Scripture quotations are taken from the King James Version (KJV) of the Holy Bible.

Editor's note: This book has been edited for the modern reader. Words, expressions, and sentence structure have been updated for clarity and readability.

GOD'S WILL: OUR DWELLING PLACE

ISBN: 0-88368-841-7
Printed in the United States of America
© 1982 by Whitaker House

Whitaker House
30 Hunt Valley Circle
New Kensington, PA 15068
web site: www.whitakerhouse.com

Library of Congress Cataloging-in-Publication Data

Murray, Andrew, 1828–1917.
  God's will : our dwelling place / Andrew Murray.
    p. cm.
  ISBN 0-88368-841-7 (pbk.)
  1. Christian life—Reformed authors. 2. God—Will. I. Title.
  BV4509.5 .M9 2002
  248.4'8—dc21

                                                    2002011648

1 2 3 4 5 6 7 8 9 10 11 12 13 14 / 11 10 09 08 07 06 05 04 03 02

Contents

Preface

Creation finds its origin, existence, happiness, power, and glory in the will of God.

Redemption also finds its origin, maintenance, blessedness, power, and glory in God's will.

The life of grace in the heart owes its origin, maintenance, blessedness, power, and its glory, as well, to the will of God.

In knowing, loving, doing, bearing, and fulfilling His blessed will, the spiritual life finds its growth, rest, joy, strength, fruitfulness, and its everlasting blessedness.

The one thing a Christian needs is to continually live in the will of God.

Whether it is God's will in His providence in time or His purpose in eternity, God's will in His precepts or His promises, he who lives there will find God Himself and all His salvation.

May God teach us that as His will is the one cause and power of all that He does to demonstrate His glory, and of all that His Son did and does for our redemption, so the one thing His child needs is to prove that his whole life is the manifestation of the power and glory of God's blessed will.

With the prayer that God, by His Holy Spirit, may reveal this to each reader of this book—Yours in Christ Jesus,

Andrew Murray

Thou sweet, beloved will of God,
    My anchor ground, my fortress hill,
My spirit's silent, fair abode,
    In Thee I hide me and am still.

Thou, that willest good alone,
    Lead Thou the way—Thou guidest best;
A little child, I follow on,
    And trusting, lean upon Thy breast.

Thy beautiful, sweet will, my God,
    Holds fast in its sublime embrace
My captive will, a gladsome bird,
    Prisoned in such a realm of grace.

Within this place of certain good,
    Love evermore expands her wings,
Or nestling in Thy perfect choice,
    Abides content with what it brings.

Oh, lightest burden, sweetest yoke,
    It lifts, it bears my happy soul,
It giveth wings to this poor heart;
    My freedom is Thy grand control.

Thy wonderful, grand will, my God,
    With triumph now I make it mine;
And faith shall cry a joyous Yes!
    To every dear command of Thine.

Chapter 1
The Glory of Heaven

"Thy will be done in earth, as it is in heaven."
—Matthew 6:10

The human will is the power by which a person determines his actions and decides what to do or not to do. His hidden, inward being, proving what his desires and dispositions are—foolish or wise, good or evil—is manifested in this will. The will is the revelation of character and life. What a person truly wills, he infallibly seeks to have done, either by himself or through others.

In the will of God, we have the perfect expression of His divine perfection. Because He is the fountain of all beauty and blessedness, His will is inconceivably beautiful and blessed. His divine wisdom and goodness are made known through it. Through it alone can man know his God. In accepting and doing God's will, man finds the only and the sure way to fellowship and union with the Father.

The glory and the blessedness of heaven consist of nothing but this—God's will is done therein and by all. There is nothing to hinder God's working His blessed will in countless hosts. Those to whom He wills goodness, blessedness, and service, surrender their whole beings in submission and adoration. God lives in them and they in God. They are filled with the fullness of God.

In the Lord's Prayer, our Blessed Master teaches us to come to the Father with the wonderful petition that His will may be done on earth, even *"as it is in heaven"*! He calls us to open our hearts and to think and lift them heavenward in real desire and prayer. He bids us to count on an answer. According to the power that He works in us, we are to expect the experience in such measure as we are fitted for: God's will done in us and by us, *"in earth, as it is in heaven."* The God who works it in heaven is our Father, and He delights to work it on earth. The blessedness of earth cannot possibly be different from that of heaven. Let our hearts desire and delight to have the will of God done.

"Thy will be done, as in heaven, so on earth!" These chapters invite you to come and meditate on this petition. In this way, the Father, by His Holy Spirit, may show you the divine beauty of His will and the altogether heavenly blessedness of living in it. Let us begin by considering what God's will includes. Then, we may know exactly what our Lord means and what we are to expect when we pray, *"Thy will be done."*

There is, first, *the will of God's holy providence.* Everything that happens on earth comes to the child of God as the will of his Father. In His infinite wisdom, God so overrules all the evil of men and devils that in permitting it, He can take it up into His will and make it work out His purpose. Joseph said of his brothers' sin: *"Ye thought evil against me; but God meant it unto good"* (Genesis 50:20). Jesus said to Pilate: *"Thou couldest have no power at all against me, except it were given thee from above"* (John 19:11). In everything that happened to Him, He saw God's will. The cup was the Father's will for Him.

When the Christian learns to see God's will in everything that happens to him—grievous or pleasing, great or small—the prayer, *"Thy will be done,"* will become the unceasing expression of adoring submission and praise. The whole world, with its dark mysteries, life, and difficulties, will be illuminated by the light of God's presence and rule. The soul will taste the rest and the bliss of knowing that it is always encircled and watched over by God's will. Nothing can separate the soul from the love of which the will is the expression. Happy is the Christian who receives everything in providence as the will of His Father.

Next, there is *the will of God's righteous precepts.* Every command of our Father in heaven is a ray of the divine will—radiant to the eye that can see it—with all the perfection of the divine nature. It comes as proof of the divine condescension, tenderly accommodating itself to our feebleness as it puts the divine will into words that we can understand. It is suited to our special capacity and circumstances.

We all naturally connect the rays of light on earth with the sun from which they come. The more the Christian learns to link every precept with the infinite will of love from which it comes, the more he will see the nobility and the joy in a life of entire obedience. The privilege and the honor of carrying out, in human forms, the perfect will of the Father in heaven will be made clear. He then learns to say of God's precepts, *"They are the rejoicing of my heart"* (Psalm 119:111). And "Thy will be done, as in heaven" becomes the secret inspiration for gladly fulfilling all God's commands.

Then comes *the will of God's precious promises.* We often fail to grasp or understand some promise because we deal with it as a part and do not connect it with the great whole of God's blessed will for us. Let every believer earnestly seek to realize what God's will in His promises is. It is His determination and desire to do a certain thing, for us or in us, if we will only trust Him. Behind the promise, the faithful, almighty God waits to fulfill it.

What strength it would give in prayer—what confidence in expectation—to be quiet and trace the promise to God's living will and loving heart. He wills to make it true to everyone who yields himself in trust and dependence. *"Thy will be done,"* in view of God's providence, is the language of a glad submission. In view of His precepts, it is the surrender to a full obedience. Here, in relation to the promises, it becomes the song of an assured hope. Your will be done, by Yourself in us, O Father in heaven.

One more thought—there is *the will of God's eternal purpose.* Our understanding of God's will in His providence, His precepts, and His promises is often very much confined to ourselves. The believer, who longs to enter fully into the entire will of God, will be led to a wider and a deeper insight into the glory of its counsels. He will learn something of that great purpose that has filled the heart of God from eternity. This purpose reveals nothing less than the triumph of God's redeeming love in a world of sin.

As he is led by the Holy Spirit into the great counsels of redemption and into the meaning of the sacrifice by which God has sought to accomplish them, the believer feels how little he has realized his position. As he comes to know the patience with which God is working out His plans and the final triumph that is so sure and so glorious, the meaning of this prayer becomes clear. *"Thy will be done in earth, as it is in heaven"* becomes the expression of his fellowship with God in the wondrous carrying out of His everlasting counsel of grace. This prayer demonstrates the believer's intercession on behalf of a perishing world and his joyful anticipation of all flesh seeing the glory of God. He feels like a piece of dust floating in the sunlight of God's presence. He knows himself an instrument, a vessel, a member of the body of Christ, through which God's glory is working out His perfect will.

Believer, come and listen. This prayer needs your whole heart. You need the teaching and the indwelling of Jesus Christ in your heart to be able to pray it correctly. This prayer calls for a heart, a will, and a life entirely given up to the Father in heaven by His indwelling Spirit before it can be understood. Let the glory of God doing His will *in* us and *through* us be met by nothing less than a will wholly given up to do His will on earth, as it is done in heaven. Study how God's will is done in heaven. Yield yourself to do it even so on earth.

Chapter 2
The Way to Heaven

"Not every one that saith unto me, Lord, Lord, shall enter into the kingdom of heaven; but he that doeth the will of my Father which is in heaven."
—Matthew 7:21

We have seen that the will of God constitutes the glory of heaven. Heaven is nothing but the unhindered manifestation of the working of God's will. It is the outshining of His hidden glory in what He does. The inhabitants of heaven owe all their glory to God's working His will of love in them. And they owe all their happiness to their working it out in His service. The petition in the Lord's Prayer teaches us to long and to ask for earth to become like heaven and for His will to be done here even as it is done there. Our text follows naturally from this truth. The only way to be fit to enter heaven is to do the will of God here on earth. Every thought of heaven that does not lead us to do the will of God is a vain imagination.

There are many Christians who have never seen this. They think that the way to heaven is found in pious desires and religious duties. They believe that trusting Christ for mercy and seeking to be kept from gross sin will secure them a place in heaven for eternity. But the thought that Christ states here—only those who love to do the will of God can enter heaven—has never taken possession of their minds or hearts.

And yet our Lord plainly points out the difference between the religion of prayer and profession and the religion of obedience and performance. "Not every one who says to me, Lord, Lord"—who prays to Me and professes to acknowledge and honor Me as Savior— "but he who does the will of my Father in heaven, he alone will enter the kingdom of heaven."

It is the Father's presence and the Father's will in heaven that make heaven what it is. Doing the Father's will on earth is the only conceivable way of entering heaven. Nothing else can give the capacity for enjoying it. There must always be harmony between a life and its environment. To enter the heaven of God's will without a nature that loves and does His will is an impossibility.

But why do so many make the terrible mistake of thinking that they are honestly longing and striving to get to heaven? Let us try to answer this question. In everything that exists, there is an outward form or shape in which it manifests itself. But there is also an inward power or life that constitutes its true nature or being. It is the same with heaven and our thought of it. Men regard it as a place full of brightness, glory, and happiness—free from all sorrow or pain, full of all that can give rest and joy.

And who would not wish to enter there? Even the most worldly people hope to find a place in it when they have to leave this present life. But they never think that what attracts them is only an external image they form of heaven. And they do not know that what constitutes the actual, essential glory of heaven—what really gives heaven and its inhabitants their rest and joy and everlasting song—is the presence of the Father who is in heaven. It is the undisturbed supremacy of His holy will. Because God's will does everything in heaven and is done by everyone there, His blessedness fills all. Oh, the folly of thinking about entering into heaven while they are utterly incapable of enjoying it! Neither the

Father in heaven, nor His will on earth just as in heaven are the desire or joy of their hearts.

The same error—mistaking the outward for the inward—is made in regard to Christianity. God's Word calls us to seek, to strive, to listen to God's truth, to pray and believe, and to forsake sin and follow after that which is good. And so men seek to put their trust in Christ, to confess Him, and to do many things in His name. And, then, they think that this is Christianity. All the while, they forget that the inner, spiritual reality of true Christianity is the knowing and loving and doing of the Father's will as their one desire and delight. They do not know that Jesus is a Savior from sin and that He must work this faith in us. They do not yet realize that this is the only proof that our faith is true. The entrance to heaven can be found by this path alone.

When this is preached, many comfort themselves with the thought of God's mercy. Did Christ just come for those who had sinned and had not done God's will? He did indeed, blessed be God! But He did not come for those who continue in sin and who do not make the will of God the object of their life. Man's sin and misery was that he had fallen out of the will of God into his own will and the will of Satan. Christ came with the one object of redeeming us from the power of our own will. He came to give us a new nature and His Holy Spirit, to enable us, here on earth, to love and do God's will. Without this, our Lord assures us that there can be no thought of our entering into heaven.

The same righteous grace that receives the ungodly into favor without works—through faith alone—will, on Judgment Day, take works into account as proof of faith in and union with Christ. They will determine if we are to enter heaven. As we are saved without works, we are created in Christ Jesus for good works—works that God had prepared beforehand and that we should walk in. Without these, there can be no entrance into heaven; they are indispensable. The Master's words are plain and decisive: He who does the will of My Father in heaven will enter into the kingdom of heaven. (Carefully study Matthew 16:27; 25:31–46; Romans 2:6–7; 2 Corinthians 5:10.)

Christ came from heaven to show us that doing the will of the Father is the one mark of a son of God. And He also came to show us that we will be saved by doing His will. True conversion is turning away from our self-will and giving ourselves to the will of God as our duty and our only blessedness. I ask every believer who reads this to inquire and ask whether he thinks that the doing of the Father's will has taken the place in his life, faith, and conduct that it did in the life, conduct, and teaching of Jesus Christ. It is the one object of Christ's salvation and the one preparation for entering heaven. Read the question over again and pause. It is worthy of careful consideration.

All salvation on earth or in heaven is doing the will of God. If we find that this blessed truth has never shone with its full, heavenly light into our souls, let us at once turn to our Lord Jesus and ask Him to teach us. Let us give ourselves up to it—to study, to believe, to practice, to rejoice in it. Let us choose the will of God—His whole will, and nothing but His will—to rule over us and dwell within us each day. The living Father whose love can make it our blessedness through the living Christ, who loves to teach it to us and work it in us, will enable us to do His will.

Chapter 3
Our Union with Jesus

*"For whosoever shall do the will of my Father
which is in heaven, the same is my brother,
and sister, and mother."*
—Matthew 12:50

How many Christians deeply long for a more intimate fellowship with the Lord Jesus! The thought of a fuller experience of His love, abiding presence, and mighty power to save from sin and self greatly attracts them. They often wonder why the longings and prayers of years appear to avail so little. They are ready to turn to anyone who they think can help them discover the secret of having the full manifestation of the love and power of Christ in their hearts. Come, my reader, turn today to our blessed Lord Himself, and let Him tell you His open secret. The way into the most intimate union with Christ is very simple—"doing the will of His Father." Of one who does this, He says, *"the same is my brother, and sister, and mother."*

What does this mean? A brother or a sister is one who is born of the same father, shares the same love, home, and care. Brothers and sisters bear, in some measure, the same likeness in disposition and character. They are bound to their other brothers and sisters by these ties in a common love and fellowship. When Christ calls one of us a brother or sister, it means nothing less. Like Him, we are born of God. The Father's life and love and likeness are in us, as in Him. As the Elder Brother, He gives us and shares with us all that He has. He pours out on us all the love with which the Father loves Him. He is not ashamed to call us brethren. He delights in our relationship to Him, in our welfare, and in our society. He lives only to find His happiness in us and in what He can do for us. The one thing He longs for is that we would know and claim our relationship—that we would come to Him and be free with Him as no brother or sister ever was.

Let us pray for the quickening of the Holy Spirit to make all this a reality. Just think of the joy the believer would experience if he truly realized this: Jesus loves me as a brother; yes, me—just as I am, unworthy and sinful. He loves me as a brother. No elder brother ever watched over a weak, younger brother as tenderly as my Elder Brother watches over me. He wants me to know it. He gives the command, *"say unto them, I ascend unto my Father, and your Father"* (John 20:17). He wants me to know it. He longs for me to live with Him as a brother in the Father's presence. He is able and willing to make the possibility a reality. He invites us to come and say in tender reverence, O my holy Elder Brother—I scarcely dare say, and yet I may and I will—I am Your brother. You are my Brother. He can enable us to realize it and to abide in His presence all day and every day.

And what is the disposition of heart that can claim the blessing and abide in it? Read again, *"For whosoever shall do the will of my Father which is in heaven, the same is my brother, and sister, and mother."* Here, the Lord reveals the deepest secret of His own life as the Son of God on earth. He came as a man to prove the blessedness and the glory of doing the will of the Father. In His human life, this was the one disposition that lay at the root of His power to conquer sin, to satisfy God, and to save us. Doing the will of God is the only possible way of pleasing Him.

Thinking as God thinks, loving what God loves, willing as God wills, doing what God says—how could we think that there is any way but this to the fellowship or the favor of

God? Of Himself, Jesus said, *"I have kept my Father's commandments, and abide in his love"* (John 15:10). The law for the Elder Brother is the unchangeable law for all the children. Doing the Father's will is the only true mark of being a child. Likewise it is the one condition for admission to the full experience of a walk in all the joy that the brotherhood of Jesus can bring. Doing the will of the Father is the bond of union with Jesus.

The converse is also true. Union with Jesus gives the power to do the will of the Father. We begin with "willing to do His will" and doing it as far as we know and can. When this is really done with the whole heart, we come and claim the promise of being admitted consciously into the love and society of the Elder Brother. In true fellowship with Him—studying His example, drinking in His Spirit, receiving His strength—we receive deeper insight and greater love of God's will. We begin to long to live in it wholly, even as Jesus did. And so we go from strength to strength. Doing the will prepares us for the brother-life, and the brother-life prepares us for the doing of the will. In ever closer union with Him, the Elder Brother imparts to us—in ever deeper measure—the secret of His own blessed life in the will of God.

And what is that secret? It is found in the words our Lord so frequently uses—*"the will of my Father which is in heaven.*" Christ was only able to do and suffer as He did because it was the will of a loving Father. The will of the Father was nothing but the experience of the love of the Father. Therefore, Christ delighted to do it and was able to do it.

Many Christians never learn to understand the difference between the law of God and the will of God. The law is given by a Ruler. When embodied in a statute book, it may be kept or broken, with very little thought of personal relationship to the Lawgiver. For this reason, the law has no power to secure obedience. Christ speaks of the will as the will of the Father—the expression of a personal, living communication, in which the Father's voice and presence is always known. The will is never for a moment separated from Him. It was the ever present love of God showing His will, and the ever blessed enjoyment of that love, that enabled Christ to be obedient even unto death. It is this alone that can enable us to do the Father's will.

As a believer seeks to know the life of a brother of the first begotten Son, he will experience and know the grace to do only the Father's will. He will receive the faith to believe that, through fellowship and the power of Christ, such a life is possible. And the joyful devotion to walk in the will of God, being led by His hand, will be made known to him.

It is indeed a change in the life of a believer when he fully grasps and experiences the difference between the law of God and the will of the Father. He sees how the only power to do the will is the unceasing experience of the Father's presence—His loving voice, His guiding eye, His inspiring love. He sees how that was the life Jesus lived, how the life Christ lives in us is nothing less. He learns to understand how doing the Father's will is the one blessing into which faith is to lead us—the one secret of abiding union with Christ Jesus.

Go out, my soul, into your work this day, and let your life be transfigured by the one thought: Like Jesus, with Jesus, in Jesus I live to do the Father's will. And when you fail, or fear to fail, just whisper, "O my Lord, my Elder Brother, You and I are one in doing the Father's will."

Chapter 4
Our Food

"I have meat to eat that ye know not of...
my meat is to do the will of him that sent me,
and to finish his work."
—John 4:32, 34

When tempted in the wilderness by Satan to satisfy His hunger by a miracle, Christ answered, *"Man shall not live by bread alone, but by every word that proceedeth out of the mouth of God"* (Matthew 4:4). The life is more than bread. God's Word, received and obeyed, is the true nourishment of our lives. In the Beatitudes, Christ said, *"Blessed are they which do hunger and thirst after righteousness: for they shall be filled"* (Matthew 5:6). And so He says here that to do the will of the Father who sent Him, and to accomplish His work, is the meat that He eats, the food by which He lives. The hidden manna is God's will. To do God's will is to eat and live. Let us think about what this eating teaches us.

Eating means the maintenance of life. All life must be supported by nourishment from without if it is to survive. And the food must always be conducive to the nature of the life it sustains and the organs that receive it. Our physical lives are fed from the life of nature. Our spiritual lives can only be maintained by the eternal life that is in God. There is no way for us to receive that life day by day except by doing the will of God. The life of God reveals and communicates itself only in His will. In its beginning, life is always a gift. But its maintenance is always connected with action and growth. It is doing God's will and accomplishing His work that will secure the Christian's daily continuance in the divine life.

Eating means appropriation. Our bodies receive the necessary elements that internally sustain their lives from the world. These can nourish us in no other way but by being taken up into our system, assimilated, and made a very part of our own selves. It is even so in the spiritual life. As we have already said, the life of God acts and manifests itself through the will of God. And it is only by truly and fully appropriating that will—taking it into our systems, wholly assimilating it, making it a part of our own beings, and doing it—that the life can be maintained in us.

The life is a hidden, spiritual mystery; the will is its concrete expression—capable of being known and accepted, or rejected. Because the will is the divine power in action, there is no other possible way of assimilating the divine will except by action on our part—by our doing it. It is not the knowledge, the admiration, or the approval of the will of God, but the doing of it, that alone feeds the heavenly life. It is only by doing that I really make it my own. "My meat is to do His will."

Eating means the renewal and increase of strength. We do not eat just enough to maintain a bare existence. We desire a sufficient amount of food, both in quantity and quality, to give us strength and vigor for our work. Doing God's will is the sure way to become strong. Many Christians seek their strength in prayer, in faith, in God's promises, or in fellowship. They complain of their feebleness. They have never learned that Christ made doing the will of the Father His meat. It was this that was rewarded with the divine strength for all He had to do. He felt that He had only one thing to do in the world—to accomplish the work for which God had sent Him. As He did it, He received new strength for what He still had to do. This is what His disciples need. The whole power of God works in His will. As I grasp and understand that will and know I am doing the very thing God desires for me, its powers work in me. Doing the will of God brings heavenly strength.

Eating means satisfaction. God has created us so that a sense of hunger impels us to seek food. It makes our partaking of it an enjoyment and a source of satisfaction. *"Bless the* L*ORD...who satisfieth thy mouth with good things; so that thy youth is renewed like the eagle's"* (Psalm 103:1, 5). *"He satisfieth the longing soul"* (Psalm 107:9). Feeding on the will of God gives this divine satisfaction. The will of God is His glory and perfection. Doing His will leads us into a wonderful fellowship and partnership with Him.

But this means more than just doing what is right or keeping the law. No, the right things may be done under the discipline of conscience or duty without bringing real satisfaction. It is only when we do it as the will of the Father—in the sense of His presence, in fellowship with Himself, and in the loving desire to please Him—that He will give nourishment, strength, and satisfaction to the soul.

There are many Christians who mourn over their meagerness and their feebleness. They study Christ's image and example. They seek in some things to be conformed to Him. Yet they find so little of either the power or the joy of living as He lived. The cause is simple. They do not feed on the food that Christ fed on. Two people may be equally healthy, but the difference in their food intake may make all the difference in their strength and success.

The believer has the same eternal life that was in Christ Jesus. But he needs the same daily food if there is to be any measure of the conformity that God expects and has provided for. Our Lord tells us, *"My meat is to do the will of him that sent me."* He who eats of this meat will have a more abundant life—will *"be satisfied as with marrow and fatness"* (Psalm 63:5).

And what is the reason for so much failure in feeding on this heavenly food? It may be that the church has not taught it as clearly as was needed. Or, it could be that we heard and did not listen. Or, it could be that when we did listen, we were deceived by Satan's lie that this was too hard a path to follow. And yet the Lord has said it so plainly: The will of God is the glory of heaven. The doing of God's will ought to be our great prayer on earth.

The doing of God's will is the only ticket to heaven—the only sign of family likeness in the home of Jesus. The doing of God's will is the only food on which a child of God can thrive and be able to accomplish the work the Father has given him to do. The doing of God's will is our daily food. We must look over our past life and see if we have been feeding on this. And if not, we must believe that a change of diet—a return to the simple, heavenly fare on which the Son of God lived His life and did His work—will restore us to health and make the work of God our joy and our life.

Soul, pray for a great hunger for the will of God—as naturally and as continually as you pray for your daily bread. Even if it is only for a crumb of this heavenly bread from the Father's table, beg God to show you His will for you and enable you to do it for Him. It may be the beginning of a change in your life. The work you have done for God, at your choice and in your way, and the commandments you have tried to obey, may all become the loving will of the living Father. They will be as living fellowship with the living God. Instead of eating the bread you had to find yourself, you will say, *"I have meat to eat that ye know not of"*—the will of the Father made known and performed day by day.

Chapter 5
The Salvation of the Perishing

"Even so it is not the will of your Father which is in heaven, that one of these little ones should perish."
—Matthew 18:14

Here, our Lord used the words *"little ones"* to refer to both children, as in verses two and three, and also feeble and immature followers, *"These little ones which believe in me"* (verse 6). He said that just as surely as a man rejoices over the recovery of one lost sheep, so the Father does not will that anyone, even the feeblest and most despised, would perish. When our Lord spoke elsewhere of His doing the Father's will, He was especially referring to the will of God to save the lost.

The will of the Father is the salvation of men. All the leadings of God's will, down to the minutest of life's details, have their roots

37

in this great fountain of redeeming love: that not even one of the little ones should perish. Christ's coming down from heaven, all His speaking and doing, His living, suffering, and dying, had its unity in this—it was the revelation of God's will to save and of Christ's surrender of Himself to do that will in saving all whom the Father had given Him.

When we yield ourselves to do the Father's will, His will must be to us what it was to Christ. The salvation of men must be the main object of our lives, the one thing we do. The life that was in Christ is the same life that is in us. The glory of the Father, the blessedness of being the channels of the Father's love, and the entire surrender to the one work the Father wants done in the world, all claim our devotion as much as they claimed that of Christ. There is an infinite difference in the part He took and the part we are to take in carrying out that will. But the will itself is to be as much the joy and the aim of our lives as it was of His. The greater our understanding of God's will, the more surely we will grow to the stature of the perfect man in Christ Jesus. And the more complete our surrender to it, in all its breadth, and the more wholly possessed of it we are, the sooner we will reach our Christian maturity.

It is here that so many Christians fail. They seek to know the will of God in only its minute details concerning themselves. They live practically under a law consisting of commandments and ordinances.

Their own personal happiness is the first thing. Obedience and sanctification are subordinate to these as the means to an end. This selfish element infects and enfeebles their entire Christianity. They have no concept of the nobility and heavenly royalty of spirit that comes to the man who forgets and loses himself to do the will of God for the salvation of men.

It was this will that sent Christ into the world. It was this will that animated Him during His whole life. It was to breathe that will into our hearts and lives that the Holy Spirit came. It is in being possessed by that will, even as Christ was possessed by it—yielding ourselves to the mastery of divine love— that the image of God is restored in us. Only then may we live solely to love and to bless, even as God does.

"It is not the will of your Father which is in heaven, that one of these little ones should perish." What inspiration these words have given to God's workers on behalf of orphans, waifs, runaways, children in India perishing from famine, and children in Africa suffocating from oppression. What courage these words have been to thousands of teachers for

the little ones of whom they had charge. What patience and strength they have breathed into the hearts of those who have had to deal with the neglected and the outcast in every land. It was their joy and hope that they knew they were doing the will of God. They knew that the mighty will of God was working itself out through them.

They all have experienced how blessed it was at times to look away from their own little and limited interests and duties and to cast themselves into that mighty stream of God's loving will—a will that is slowly but surely working out His blessed purpose. There they found themselves in fellowship with God's own Son. They communed with the saints of all ages, whose one glory had been knowing and fulfilling the redeeming will of God.

What a change it would bring into the lives of many believers to know and love *this* will of the Father. How glorious to lose self and sacrifice all in order to be mastered and consumed by its blessed fire. If you want to know it as such and be possessed by it, you must make it a definite object of study and desire. Seek to acquire a proper impression of its glory through prayer and meditation. Ask the Holy Spirit to give you a spiritual vision of the infinite energy of the divine love, as it wills nothing but good to every one of its creatures.

The Salvation of the Perishing

The divine love needs time and thought and prayer. It needs the giving up of all our self-satisfaction with our limited views of God's will. It needs an open, thirsty heart longing to be filled with the fullness of God and His will if we are to have this will of love dwell in us and possess us. It needs, above all, the indwelling of Christ—in whom that will is realized and manifested—to make us partakers of His own Spirit and disposition. We then can know something of that infinite will of love working itself out through us. It shall fill the little vessel of our will out of its own living stream and make the will of God, indeed, our will.

We have seen that it is doing the will of God that is the glory and way to heaven, our likeness to the Elder Brother, and the food of our spiritual life. Let us begin doing the will of God in this aspect too, really giving ourselves to Him for this saving of the lost. It will awaken within us our capacity to better understand the glory of the divine will—that none of the little ones would perish. And the divine privilege of our being is to be made partakers of the will of God. There is no other way for us to enter into fellowship with God but to have one will with Him. And there is no way to this except through Christ and the participation of His Spirit. As we intelligently grasp who and what Christ is, understand His true life as the Son who came and gave himself up to work out the Father's will and love, and accept no one other than Him as our Lord and our life, hope will arise that this redeeming will can master us too, as its vessels and channels. We, too, can go through the world filled with a divine life. The divine will can inspire and energize our will, and life may pass out through us to those who are perishing.

Chapter 6
Not Mine Own Will

"I can of mine own self do nothing: as I hear, I judge: and my judgment is just; because I seek not mine own will, but the will of the Father which hath sent me."
—John 5:30

The will of God is the power by which the universe exists from moment to moment. It is by the unceasing, active exercise of His will that the sun shines and every lily is clothed with beauty. There is no goodness, strength, or beauty, except as He wills it. The glory and blessedness of heaven are nothing but the working of His will. The hosts of heaven live with their wills turned and opened to Him. They find their happiness in allowing His will to do its perfect work in them.

When the Blessed Son became man to lead us to God, He told us that the whole secret of His life was not doing His own will, but rather, yielding Himself to do the will of the Father. In this way, His will would receive and work out that which the will of the Father worked in Him. He had been sent—and was delighted to come—for the sole purpose of doing the will of the Father, with His human will and His human body. He was to be our model of a man, a true man, finding His blessedness and His way to God's glory in the absolute surrender to God's will. He thus showed us the destiny that man was created for and the new life He was to bring His people.

In such entire dependence on God—doing nothing of Himself, judging nothing except as the Father directed—He was always able to give a righteous judgment. He could count on God to give Him all the wisdom and the strength He needed to work out His own will perfectly in Him. All for the one simple reason: *"Because I seek not mine own will, but the will of the Father which hath sent me."*

"Not mine own will, but the will of the Father which hath sent me." But does this mean that our Lord Jesus had a will different from the Father's? Did He have a will that needed to be denied? Undoubtedly. But was not such a will sin? By no means. The fact that man has a self hood, an own will, a power of self-determination by which he is to decide what he should be, is the glory of

his creation. Man's having his own desire and thought and will is not sin. Without this, he could not be a free being. He has a will so that he may decide whether he should act according to the will of God or not. Sin enters in only when man adheres to his own will, rather than the will of God.

As a man, made like us in all things, *"in all points tempted like as we are, yet without sin"* (Hebrews 4:15), Christ had a human will. For instance, He ate when He was hungry, and He shrank from suffering when He saw it coming. We know how, in the temptation in the wilderness, He kept the former; and in the prospect of His death, He kept the latter. In both, He remained in perfect subjection to the Father's will. (See Matthew 4:4; Luke 12:50; John 12:27.) It is this that gives infinite worth to His sacrifice. It was the unceasing sacrifice of His human will to the Father that was of value. *"I seek not mine own will, but the will of the Father which hath sent me."*

These words reveal the innermost meaning of Christ's redemption. They teach us about the life that we were created for and out of which we fell in Paradise. They show us what the sinfulness of that fallen state consists of and that Christ came to deliver us. He seeks to free us from our self-will. They reveal the true human-life and the true Son-life— perfect oneness of will with God's will. They open the secret power of Christ's redeeming work—atoning for our self-will by His loyalty at all costs to God's will. They divulge the true nature of the salvation and the life He gives us—the will and the power to say, *"I delight to do Your will, O God"* (Psalm 40:8).

Every spirit seeks a form in which to embody itself. These words give the highest revelation of the life in which the Spirit that was in Christ embodied itself in Him. And the Spirit embodies itself in all who truly and fully seek to accept His salvation to the utmost. "I seek not my will, but the will of the Father who sent me," is the keynote of the only life that is well-pleasing to the Father on earth. It is the only way to prepare for His fellowship in heaven.

How little God's children know the Christ He has given them. And how little they realize the true nature of the salvation that Christ came to bring. How very many have never been taught that salvation out of self-will into doing God's will alone is true blessedness. And how many who, if they think they know it as a truth, never seek this first as the true entrance into the kingdom of God and His righteousness. And yet this is in very deed what Christ revealed, promised, secured on Calvary, and bestowed from heaven in the Holy Spirit. How can we possess this blessed life?

I have previously pointed out the great difference between the law of a state, as contained in a statute book, and the will of a king to whom one stands in a personal relationship. If we truly desire to follow, however distantly, in Christ's footsteps, we must stand with Him in the same close, personal relationship to the Father. Without this, the most earnest efforts to do the Father's will must prove a failure. When our Lord so often spoke of *"the will of my Father, which is in heaven"* (Matthew 12:50), He wanted us to understand that it was the living personality and love that was His motive and power for obedience. When He spoke of *"the will of the Father which hath sent me,"* He showed that it was not only the awareness of having a purpose, but the desire of pleasing the One who sent Him; that was the mainspring of all He did.

We need a sense of the presence and nearness of the God whose will we are to do as much as our Lord needed that sense. Separate the thing you have to do from Him whose will it is, and it becomes a burden and an impossibility. Live in the faith that He has sent you. It is His living, loving will—which He watches over, which He Himself even works out—that you are doing. Instead of being a burden you are to carry, it becomes a power that carries you. The will of the Father is such a beautiful, wise, gentle, loving will; to know

47

it as the breathing out of the heart of God makes it an infinite attraction and delight.

And how can we enter into this experience of the Father's nearness and thus be able to do everything as His will? There is only one way: Jesus Christ must work it in us. And that not as from without, strengthening our faculties or assisting our efforts. No, this blessed doing of the Father's will is the mark of His life as Son. He can work it in us, as we yield ourselves wholly and receive Him truly to dwell in us. It is right and necessary that we set ourselves with all earnestness and make the attempt. It is only by failure that we really learn how entirely He must and will do all. So inseparably is this *"seek*[ing] *not mine own will, but the will of the Father which hath sent me"* connected with Jesus Christ, that it is only when He comes in and manifests Himself in the heart and dwells there that He can work this full salvation in us. *"Blessed are they which do hunger and thirst after righteousness: for they shall be filled"* (Matthew 5:6).

Chapter 7
Doing, the Way to Knowing

"If any man will do his will, he shall know of the doctrine, whether it be of God, or whether I speak of myself."
—John 7:17

There was great division among the Jews as to who Christ really was and the divine authority of the truth He taught. They wanted some sign as clear proof that He had really come from God. Christ's answer told them that the proof depended on the state of their hearts.

A man who wants the divine evidence of Christ's mission while he is not ready to do God's will seeks for it in vain. A man whose will is set on doing God's will, as far as he knows it, is alone in the proper state for receiving further divine illumination.

God's Will: Our Dwelling Place

Our Lord said, *"If any man will do his will, he shall know of the doctrine, whether it be of God."* He spoke of two things: the will of God we are to do, and the teaching about God we are to know. He told us that the second is entirely dependent upon the first. As we will to do, we shall be able to know. This is the contrast and the connection between precept and promise. Will—be ready, be determined—to fulfil God's purpose, and you shall have divine light and certainty as to all that Jesus has taught. The commands are simple and easily understood. He who honestly seeks to do them in the fear of God will learn to know the mystery of Christ. A will, a disposition set on doing God's will, is the only way to know God's truth.

There are many Christians who complain about their lack of spiritual discernment. The promises of Christ in this very gospel of John appear beyond their reach. They would love to know that "the teaching is of God." They would like to experience and to feel that it is of divine origin and with divine effectiveness. They want to know that God Himself confirms and makes the words true as a living power. In this chapter, Christ promises streams of living water flowing out of the believer. Later on, He promises a more abundant life. He vows that His followers will not walk in darkness, but that they have the light of life and will do greater works than He had done. He promises to manifest Himself to us, to dwell in us along with the Father. It is His pledge that we will abide in Him and He in us. We may ask what we will, and He has promised to give it to us.

When a man really knows a teaching is from God—it has the truth and power of God in it—it becomes easy for him to believe, and he receives its fulfillment. To all believers who really long to have these promises shine with divine light in their hearts, Christ's message comes today: It all depends on whether or not you really will to do the will of God. Let us try to take hold of the lessons we need.

Christ teaches us that, in the growth of the Christian life, faith depends upon character. Just as, at conversion, there can be no faith without repentance, so also, throughout life, faith cannot grow or inherit the promises without a life given up to the doing of God's will. Some, having thrust from themselves a good conscience, have made a shipwreck of the faith. (See 1 Timothy 1:19.) The great reason that so many pray for an increase of faith and never get it is that the will to fulfil his purpose has never taken the place it must have. The will rules the life and is the index of the heart. The whole man is to be judged by the will. Unless there is a fixed resolve—a seeking with the whole will to do the will of

God—there can be no growth in faith and no knowledge of the divine truth to which it gives access. It is only as God's will is truly and fully taken up into my willing and doing that God can reveal Himself to me.

God judges our conduct by the will. Our Lord says, *"If any man will do His will."* A believer may, in his youth, through ignorance or feebleness, fail in doing God's will. If he searches his heart and sees that he indeed wills, longs, and thirsts to do it, God shall see that he is ready for spiritual light. *"If there be first a willing mind, it is accepted according to that a man hath, and not according to that he hath not"* (2 Corinthians 8:12). A believer, as in Romans 7, may be able to say that he delights in the law of God after the inward man, and yet has to mourn his terrible failure. If there really is this will to do, his failure shall lead him on to see how Romans 8:2–4 is the deliverance from the law of sin in the members by the law of the Spirit of life in Christ Jesus. Then, the righteousness of the law is fulfilled in those who walk after the Spirit.

Christ's words are not meant for those who are content with the idea that they *will* to do God's purpose, while they do not also press on to the life in the Spirit that God works both to will and to do. It is the heart where the will is needed—with its whole strength set on God's will—so that the divine truth and power of Christ's teaching will be known. To do the will of God, the first step is thus to take it up into our will. The will of God is the heavenly treasure in the earthen vessel of our will. The excellency of the power is of God and not of us. And so we learn to trust God to work His own will in us and through us.

I cannot too frequently or too earnestly repeat this message: The one object for which our will was given us—its true nobility and blessedness—is that with it we might take in God's will and make it our very own. Before I can see all that that will implies or feel that I have the power to perform it, I must regard it as the one thing God asks from me. The one thing I can do to please Him and become a partaker of His blessedness day by day is to accept, to worship, to will to do His blessed purpose, and then to do it. He works in us both to will and to do.

Willing to do the will of God is the sure way to all growth in spiritual knowledge and experience. Actually, doing all that is within the reach of my spiritual stature and willing with the whole heart to do all that still appears beyond me is the only way to ensure that the whole body is full of divine light. The main reason why so much Bible study and prayer for divine guidance is fruitless is this—the heart is not in the right state for receiving

God's teaching. Peter wrote, *"Ye have purified your souls in obeying the truth"* (1 Peter 1:22). It is actually doing God's will—entirely surrendering to God to do it wholly and unceasingly, in the greatest things and in the least—which purifies the soul and inherits the promise, *"Blessed are the pure in heart, for they shall see God"* (Matthew 5:8).

In the will of God, there is such a divine vitality and energy that it becomes life and strength to the heart that wills *and does it.* But it must be done not merely as a matter of duty or Christian training, but because God has willed it—as God wills it. The spiritual knowledge of God, His presence, His power, and His indwelling is given to the obedient. *"If a man love me, he will keep my words: and my Father will love him, and we will come unto him, and make our abode with him"* (John 14:23).

Here is the way to a strong and joyful spiritual life. Unite yourself to the will of God. It shall unite you to Him, and it shall draw Him to you. Will, with all your will, what God has purposed. Make this the chief exercise of your spiritual life. As much as you truly have of God's will, you have of God. Our Lord said, *"I am the way, the truth, and the life"* (John 14:6). He was this because He came not to do His own will, but the will of the Father. This is the one way in which He will lead you. The new and living way He opened up in His blood was by doing God's will. This is the one truth He will be to you: Union with Him is perfected by doing the Father's will. This is the one life He will give you—the life of God given in Christ, revealed and perfected by the will of God, as it is willed and done by us.

Chapter 8
Even unto Death

"Father, if thou be willing, remove this cup from me: nevertheless not my will, but thine, be done."
—Luke 22:42

Gethsemane—the innermost sanctuary of the life of our Lord and of His great redemption. In some respects, it is even more mysterious than Calvary. The garden opens up the inner meaning and power of the visible suffering and sacrifice on the cross. And, of all the suffering of Gethsemane, *"Not my will, but thine, be done"* was the key. It shows us which sin it was that made the great sacrifice a necessity—our self-will. It reveals which disposition it was that gave the sacrifice its value—the surrender of the human will to receive God's will. The redemption that it effected was the conquest and atonement of our self-will. And the salvation it actually brings is the impartation of a will entirely given up to God.

Come, my soul; be still, and worship in holy fear as you see what it cost your Lord to speak the words you so easily say. Learn from Him about the fullness of meaning and blessing that may be found in them.

The Sin Christ Dies for

Why is the Son of God on His way to the death of the cross? What is it that causes Him all this agony and suffering? It is sin that needs this sacrifice. It is to take away sin that He is here. And the first part of His work in taking it away is that He Himself must resist and conquer it. It is this death-struggle with sin that cost Him the agony. All through His life, He had been *"in all points tempted like as we are, yet without sin"*(Hebrews 4:15). In this last hour, the powers of darkness make one great assault on the very citadel of His being. They seek to tempt Him with the sorest of all temptations—following His own will as His nature drew back from the awful curse-bearing that was set before Him.

The scene reveals what the deepest root of all sin is—the assertion of our self-will. This was the sin and the fall of Adam. This is the source of all evil on earth. This is, in the believer, the hidden cause of all failure and disappointment. God's will is the living power through which His love communicates itself and its blessings to mankind. Man's will was meant to be the power by which he was to intelligently yield himself and cooperate with God in receiving and appropriating all the divine nature had to impart.

Self-will—a will not yielded to God—is the only thing that hinders God in revealing and communicating His blessedness to man. The Cross is the proof of man's self-will, because man's will refused to bow to God's Son. Christ's agony in Gethsemane proves that it is this same sin He came to conquer and cast out.

The Victory Christ Won

We often look upon the suffering of Christ—with His endurance of the curse and death of the cross—as the source of our salvation. Scripture teaches us to look at what gave that suffering and death its inner value—Christ's obedience. It was not merely in what He did or suffered, but in the spirit in which He acted, that the cross's infinite worth—its atoning merit—is to be found. During His whole life, Christ had spoken of not doing His own will. Here, He proved that He would do the will of the Father even though it cost Him His life.

Even to the point of death, He said, "Not my will!" And so through death, in dying to His own will, He taught us what God claims as His right. The entire losing and giving up of our will and life to God's will, as the way into the life and glory of God, alone brings us to the true place of blessing.

The Atonement Christ Accomplished

And how does the victory of Christ over man's self-will profit and save us? In two ways—as we regard Him in His substitution or in His fellowship; as the Christ *for* us or as the Christ *in* us. In the first of these aspects, His victory over sin as self-will, His obedience unto death, and His infinite acceptability in the Father's sight become ours the moment we believe in Him.

As those who are united to Him by faith, His righteousness and merit—with all the Father's delight in Him because of them—are made our very own. *"We* [are] *made the righteousness of God in Him"* (2 Corinthians 5:21). The sin of our self-will is blotted out. We are dealt with by God as if we had never sinned. We are counted as righteous and allowed to look up to God in His Beloved Son as altogether pleasing to Him. If only there was a real sense of the awfulness of the sin of self-will especially in God's redeemed children—then the joy of the assurance of its being blotted out

60

would be gladly welcomed. And how fervently we would long to fully know the fruit of the victory that Christ has achieved for us in freeing us from its power as well as its guilt.

The Salvation Christ Bestows

This is the second aspect of Christ's victory—He has freed us from the dominion of self-will. The very nature and essence of the salvation He imparts is that which was also the very nature and essence of His own life—a delight and power to do God's will alone. Gethsemane teaches us how to receive the full experience of the deliverance.

Just as Christ, in His holy, sinless nature, learned obedience through what He suffered, so too the believer, who seeks to follow his Lord in full conformity, will learn what it is to know that he is crucified with Christ and dead to self and its will. Christ's learning culminated in His surrender of His will unto death. This should stir a great deal of growth in the knowledge of what Christ has won for us—both in insight into the absolute necessity of giving up all self-will, even in the least things, and also the divine certainty of God's working in us. But there can be no thought of our understanding or attaining this until we desire to give up all, even unto death, to live in the will of God alone.

Believer, is this the very Christ you delight in, seek to be conformed to, and long to know more fully in His indwelling power? In Gethsemane, He entered into the very deepest and nearest fellowship with you in surrendering His will to death. Enter into the deepest and nearest fellowship with Him in surrendering your will as He did. Pray for the Holy Spirit to show you how self-will is the root of all sin and temptation and darkness. Pray for the knowledge of how the will of God can come in, cast self-will out, and live in you. Learn how faith in Christ, who died to conquer our self-will and now waits to dwell in us, can make you partaker of His death and victory. Learn the lesson that death to self-will just means a quiet bowing before God in utter poverty and helplessness. It is simply trusting in the Blessed Lamb of God—who passed through death as the only way to the perfect surrender of His will to God's will—to breathe His own Spirit, and the very will of God, into us.

To a soul longing to live only and wholly in the will of God, death to all self-will is the one inevitable demand. But also, in the faith of Christ Jesus, it is the one sure and most blessed deliverance.

Chapter 9
Lord, What Wilt Thou?

"And he trembling and astonished said, Lord, what wilt thou have me to do?"
—Acts 9:6

The prayer, *"Thy will be done in earth, as it is in heaven"* (Matthew 6:10), needs to be followed by the more special one, *"Lord, what wilt thou have me to do?"* Men have often wondered about the secret of the wonderful consecration and power in the life of Paul. His first act at his conversion, after he knew the Lord who had met him, was the surrender of his will. *"Lord, what wilt thou have me to do?"* That word was the beginning, the root, the strength, and the mark of his whole wonderful life. His word was so blessed and fruitful because he remained faithful to the one thing: He lived only for the will of his Lord.

There are many lessons that these words suggest. The Lord has a will, a life-plan for each of us, according to which He wishes us to live. To each of us, the Lord will unfold this will or life-plan. He expects us to wait on Him for the discovery of His will—both in what is universal, for all His people, and in what He wills for each one individually. When this prayer is honest and true, it implies the wholehearted willingness to yield ourselves and our life to the doing of that will. We may count on an answer to such prayer, because God does not ask more of His child than He makes known as His will. These, and other such lessons, offer abundant occasion for meditation and prayer. In this chapter, I want to direct your attention to another lesson as well. It seems apparently simple, and yet it is of deep significance. It is what was suggested in the opening paragraph: True conversion is nothing but a surrender to live only to do the will of God.

Do not say, "But is this not obvious?" Far from it. Most Christians have never understood it. It may be that you have never yet fully grasped it. True conversion is the turning from my own will, so as never to seek or do it again. It is the surrender of my will, with all its strength, and at all times, to only seek and do that which God wills. But am I then to have no will of my own? You are indeed to

64

have a will—the stronger the better. And you are to use it with all your strength for the one great work that God created and prepared it to carry out. That one thing was to accept and to will what God wills. This is the image and likeness of God for which man was created. It is the glory and the blessedness of the life of a child of God that he can say, "The holy, heavenly, perfect will of God is my will. I have seen it and accepted it and made it my own." To will and to do with all my strength what God wills and does, this is the noblest work the will of a man can be engaged in. In this is found the very image and likeness of God: to will ever as He wills. We then learn to say, "How wonderful, what an honor; I always will just what God wills." Or as an old saint expressed it, "I am always happy, because I always have my own way. God's will and mine are always one."

This surrender to the will of God—the key of Paul's conversion and his life—is the secret of all true conversion and true Christian living. And it is because so many have accepted Christ without any understanding of God's demand that they cease from all self-will and only do His will, that they do not mature in faith and assurance. It is as if they *went backward, and not forward*" (Jeremiah 7:24). They have never understood what Scripture says of God's children. They are *"born, not of blood, nor of the will of the flesh, nor of the will of man, but of God"* (John 1:13); *"it is not of him that willeth...but of God that showeth mercy"* (Romans 9:16); *"of his own will begat he us with the word of truth"* (James 1:18).

The whole will of man, as his own power, however good and Christian it may be, is shut out of the kingdom of heaven. It has to be denied and crucified; how much more the sinful self-will. As God's will alone brought forth the divine life in us, our whole growth and our strength are to be found in it alone. *"My meat is to do the will of him that sent me"* (John 4:34). The soul's greatest hindrance in the doing of God's will is this one thing: We have not given up our will. Once a child of God begins to see that this is the defect of his Christian life, he will find no deliverance until he reaffirms his faith and confesses the one cause of failure. He was not aware of how utterly evil his will was and how entire his renunciation of it was to be. When the Lord Jesus said, *"If any man will come after me, let him deny himself, and take up his cross"* (Matthew 16:24), it meant that he should first of all deny his own will—crucify it.

The will of God is our salvation, not only as it is willed by Him, but also as it is received into our innermost beings. We must truly will to have it, submit to it, and allow it to be worked out in our lives. Because our salvation rests continually in the saving will of God, we can only have as much of His salvation as we have of His will. Until this is grasped, the true reason for our failure will not be understood. As the error and the sin are heartily acknowledged, the soul is prepared to make a new beginning. In the redeeming power of the glorified Lord Jesus, he may say to God, "I come, as it is written in the volume of the book, not only for Christ, but for each of His disciples. I delight to do Your will, O my God."

If I am to turn to God in a new and full surrender to His will, it must be in a new and full trust in what Christ can do for me. Saul's question, *"Lord, what wilt thou have me to do?"* was preceded by another: *"Who art thou, Lord?"* (Acts 9:5). It was the vision of the Son of God in His glory—the personal revelation, *"I am Jesus whom thou persecutest"* (verse 5)—that brought about the mighty change. It caused him to yield himself so readily and so entirely to the will of his newfound Lord. We need something of the same. Nothing less than a new revelation of the divine authority can come to claim and make us faithful servants of His will. Nothing except the tender love of Him whom we have grieved so long can truly enable us to say, "Lord, what will You have me do? Speak Lord, Your servant wills to do it."

Who is ready to enter on this path of entire devotion to the will of God? It is the only true Christ-life. The steps are simple.

Remember, the will of God is the revelation of His hidden, divine love and blessedness. And the only way to know and enjoy God and His love is to do His will. Therefore, boldly say, "I may, I will do nothing but God's will."

Believe that God will answer because of the prayer, *"Lord, what wilt thou?"* Jesus Christ will make God's will known day by day. And where He teaches me to know it by His Spirit, He gives me the strength to do it.

And when I have said, "Lord, here am I, ready to do all Your will," let me wait on Him to reveal Himself as my redeeming Lord. Along with the command, He gives the power.

His voice, His presence, and His love compel a willing obedience. It is the answer to the first prayer, *"Who art thou, Lord?"* that prepares us for the answer to the second, *"Lord, what wilt thou have me to do?"* Paul had heard Stephen speak of *"the Son of man standing on the right hand of God"* (Acts 7:56). It was when, in *"a light from heaven, above the brightness of the sun"* (Acts 26:13), he had this vision of the Glorified One for himself, that his eyes and heart were forever darkened to earth. It was then that his life was given up to do the will of his Lord alone. It is so even still. The faith of Christ Triumphant looking upon us and conquering us for Himself compels and empowers us to do His will alone.

Lord, show Yourself to me; then I can do whatever You ask of me. In living communion with You, I can do all things.

Chapter 10
The Man After God's Own Heart

"I have found David the son of Jesse, a man after mine own heart, which shall fulfil all my will."
—Acts 13:22

Of these two expressions in which God refers to David, we more often hear the first, *"a man after mine own heart."* The use of the second, *"who shall fulfil all my will,"* is much less frequent. And yet, it is no less important than the other. *"A man after mine own heart"* speaks of the deep, unseen mystery of the pleasure a man can give to God in heaven. *"Who shall fulfil all my will"* deals with the life down here on earth that can be seen and judged by men.

Let us seek and try to understand the truth that it is the man who does all God's will who is the man after His own heart. God seeks such men. When He finds them, He rejoices over them with great joy. They are the very men He needs—men He can trust and use. His heart, with its hidden, divine perfections, reveals itself in His will. He who seeks and loves and does all His will is a man altogether after His own heart. He is the man of absolute surrender to God's will.

In this way, David was in striking contrast with Saul. Saul was like a half-hearted and self-pleasing Christian. We know what remarkable experiences Saul had at the beginning of his life. The Spirit of God came upon him, another heart was given him, and he prophesied. (See 1 Samuel 10:10.) A sense of humility was not lacking in him. When he was to be presented to the people, he hid himself. And, speedily, God began to work salvation in Israel through him. But it was not long before self-will began to show itself. When God sent him with the command to completely destroy Amalek, he did God's work deceitfully. Under the pretense of bringing sacrifices to offer to God, he did his own will in the matter of Agag and the best of the spoil. His terrible failure was used by God to point out even more strikingly this great truth. The man whom God can use to rule His people and establish His kingdom—the man after His own heart, who pleases Him—is he of whom God can say, "He will do all My will."

After what we have already learned about God's will—the place it has in the Christian life and its preparation for a spiritual understanding of the further teaching of God's Word—it may be wise to use these words for the simplest possible instruction to those searching for the truth. What must I do so that God can say of me, *A man after mine own heart, which shall fulfil all my will*?

First of all, remember, *you cannot attain to this by anything you do.* No resolution, no effort, and no help that you seek in prayer to strengthen your weakness will bring about what you desire. And why not? Because your nature is completely ruled by self-will and totally opposed to God's will. Nothing can delight in God's will and actually do it except a new and divine nature—born and daily renewed in you by a divine power from above. *"The carnal mind is enmity against God"* (Romans 8:7), and it is in opposition to His will. The deliverance of the new nature from self and its will must be as entire as the perversion of the old nature from God and His will. Here is our first lesson: No desire, however honest; no purpose, however fixed; no surrender, however absolute, can make a man after God's own heart, a man who will do all His will. Such a man must be born from above

73

and must do all he does in the power of that new, divine life. A regenerate man may indeed, in some things, do God's will. They will be the fruit of the first, half-unconscious workings of the Holy Spirit within him. But this is only preparatory to what God really aims at—that His child, of his own free will, would intelligently and heartily choose to do *all* His will. That little word *all is* the secret of true consecration, of a life *"worthy of the Lord unto all pleasing"* (Colossians 1:10), and of being a man after God's own heart.

We all know the great difference between a feeble child, or a sickly man, and one in full health. And so, it is not enough that you just have a beginning or small measure of spiritual life. That will not enable you to do all of God's will. The question is whether you are living only, and doing all, under the power of the Holy Spirit, as the strength of the new life. It is only the Spirit of God Himself who can do the will of God.

The great reason why God's children do not claim or yield themselves, by the Spirit of God, to work all His will in them is that they do not know how foolish it is to attempt to do His will without the aid and instruction of the Spirit. Even the regenerate man is helpless to do God's will without the direct and unceasing operation of God's Spirit. Another reason is because they do not know the subtle and altogether unconquerable power of our corrupt nature, unless God Himself, through His Son and Spirit, lives and works in the innermost recesses of their being and inspires all its powers. If you learn the first lesson well—the secret aversion of your nature to God's will and your complete inability to overcome or to change it—you are ready to go on to the second.

It is this: *Believe that you have a new and divine nature, expressly designed and prepared to do all God's will.* If you remain in close and continual dependence on the Holy Spirit, through whom God in Christ works in you, you will experience this lesson as a promise from God. Jesus Christ could do nothing of Himself, though He was the Son, without the Father working in Him. Does it displease you to be as absolutely dependent on God as He was? As part of your faith in Jesus Christ, believe that God works in you as in Him. Believe this, however dark and inadequate you feel, just as you believe that at night the sun is shining on the other half of the world and will rise upon you in the morning. It is this faith, along with the humble, patient, dependent surrender to God that it works, that will bring you to an entirely new position and power in doing God's will.

In this faith, here is our third and final lesson: *Humbly but confidently give yourself up to God to do all His will.* Give yourself to Him, as a loving Father, so that you do not take His commands as mere law, but as loving will. The will of the Father will be made known to you in the loving fellowship shared between Himself and yourself. Look at God's will as one great whole—the revelation of His loving purpose for man and for you. Set yourself resolutely, in the faith of the Holy Spirit's working in you, to make it your one business to do all God's will every day. Then, again, bow yourself in the deepest humility to wait on God to work in you.

To obtain a new entrance into the kingdom of heaven, you must possess the humility that bows in deep grief at the evil nature against God's will, a soul that confesses the inability of the regenerate nature to do that will by itself, and a sense of childlike dependence that waits on God to work His will. The Christian life will become something quite new to you under the power of these great truths. You are utterly and ever abidingly unable to do God's will—even as a regenerate man—without the unceasing work of the Holy Spirit. You need divine and complete sufficiency in Christ to do all that the Father asks of you when He calls you to be a man after His own heart—a man who will do all His will.

Chapter 11

The Will of the Lord Be Done

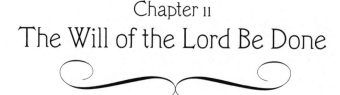

"And when [Paul] would not be persuaded,
we ceased, saying, The will of
the Lord be done."
—Acts 21:14

Paul was at Caesarea, on his way to Jerusalem. Agabus, a prophet, had said by the Holy Spirit that Paul would there be bound and delivered into the hands of the Gentiles. Paul's friends begged him not to go. In his answer, he spoke the noble words, *"I am ready not to be bound only, but also to die at Jerusalem for the name of the Lord Jesus"* (Acts 21:13). When they heard this, they said, *"The will of the Lord be done"* (verse 14). It was no longer a question of Jews or Gentiles, nor even of the life or death of Paul. If it was to be, they would accept it as the will of God. The story teaches us the wisdom, the duty, and the blessing of accepting disappointment or trial that cannot be averted as God's will. Thus, what would naturally cause sorrow or anger turns into an occasion of holy resignation and humble worship of God in His sovereign wisdom and power.

There is a twofold will of God: the will of approval and the will of permission. In the former, we see what He desires or ordains as right and good. The latter includes all that happens in the world, either as the result of natural law and secondary causes, or as the work of ungodly men and evil spirits. To admit that what God's will directly appoints is good is comparatively easy. But to recognize His will in all the evil that comes to us or around us from evil men is a truth many believers never accept. It is one of the most blessed lessons to learn that no possible trouble can ever come to us that is not the will of our Father.

Though Judas, Caiaphas, and Pilate sinned against God's holy and righteous will in the death of Jesus, He accepted the suffering and death they caused Him as the will of God. It was the cup the Father had given Him. The sin of those who persecute or hurt a child of God is not His will. And yet the suffering caused, with all its consequences, is to him God's will. As this is seen, the believer turns his eyes from the human cause and looks to the heavenly Father's will. There he finds that suffering becomes a blessing. And no power on earth or in hell can rob the soul of the perfect rest found in that blessed will. The place of trial becomes the place of blessing. Let us see what is needed to secure this.

1. In time of trial, let me say at once: *Here I am by the will of God, in the very place God has chosen for me.* Whether the trial comes from the hatred of an enemy, the wrong of a friend, through my own fault, or in the course of God's more direct providence, I may be sure that the difficulty or distress that I am in is the will of God concerning me. I, therefore, ought to heartily consent to this truth. Whether it is some great trial, some petty annoyance, a temporary grief, or some long-continued cause of weariness or irritation, be sure that the secret of peace and rest is to say, "This trouble is what God wills for me. This is what lifts me from man to God and His will. To that will I have yielded myself. In that will I rest. The will of the Lord be done."

2. This prepares the soul to say with confidence: *God, who has brought me into this trouble, will assuredly give me the grace to bear it correctly.* The grace needed to bear suffering as God wants His child to—so as to glorify Him in it—must come from Him. He will work the quiet submission,

childlike trust, and living entrance into and union with His will, in the soul that adoringly says, *"The will of the Lord be done."* The fulfillment of all the promises in Holy Scripture—with all the comfort they give in the assurance of God's presence and aid in trouble—depends entirely on the soul being given up to God's will. Then, we can prove that God's will is love and blessing. The more willingly I say, "God brought me here," the more confidently I can say, "He has charge and cares for me."

3. We will then be led farther on to the assurance: *God Himself will teach me the lessons for which He sent the trial.* This is more than the trust, peace, and surrender we have just been speaking of. They keep us from grieving God or vexing ourselves in the school of affliction. But beyond these graces, God has special lessons for every child whom He leads aside in His loving chastisement. He wants to cure us permanently of our self-will and worldliness. He wants to awaken us to the true imitation of the humility and the self-sacrifice of His Son. He desires to draw us into full fellowship with Him who made us for His divine indwelling and operation within us. He delights in fitting us to live lives of blessing to others. These lessons

are often sadly missed by those who suffer much. And those who try to learn them often feel how greatly they have failed. It is because we do not believe. The Father, who brought me into this place of trial, will Himself teach the lessons He wants me to learn. He will work all the grace He would gladly see in me. *"The will of the Lord be done"* includes not only the trial itself, but also encompasses all that God meant by it and has undertaken Himself to work out in the willing, waiting soul.

4. When we have thus entered into living union with the Father through His will, we will not fear to say: *God's will, which brought me here, can, in His way and time, bring me out again.* With many children of God, the desire for deliverance from trouble is the first, if not the only, thought. This should not be so. Suffering is not natural to us. We are at liberty to call on God for deliverance in the day of trouble. But it is not for this reason alone that the heart must turn to God.

The first desire must be that God may be glorified in loving submission and child-like teachableness. In this way, His will in all it means and aims at with the trial may be done. It is when the prayer—*"the will of the Lord be done"*—rises from the heart, in its true and full meaning, that the burden may be taken away without our being the losers. Then, the deliverance may bring as much glory to God in our holy devotion as the suffering could have done. Union with God's will will teach us how to look to it in the right spirit for help.

What a privilege that the darkest trials, the bitterest sorrows, as well as the smaller disappointments and passing fears of life can all help to unite me more perfectly with the will of my God. By His grace, I will seek to live every day amid tears of sorrow and songs of joy, in quiet submission or in triumphant faith, as they do in heaven. The one word in my heart will be, *"The will of the Lord be done."* It is this that gives heaven on earth.

> I worship Thee, sweet Will of God,
> And all Thy ways adore,
> And every day I live I seem
> To love Thee more and more.
>
> I have no cares, O blessed Will!
> For all my cares are Thine;
> I live in triumph, Lord for Thou
> Hast made Thy triumphs mine.
>
> Man's weakness waiting upon God,
> Its ends can never miss;
> For man on earth no work can do,
> More angel-like than this.

The Will of the Lord Be Done

He always wins who sides with God,
  To him no chance is lost;
God's will is sweetest to him when
  It triumphs at his cost.

Ill that He blesses is our good,
  And unblest good is ill,
And all is right that seems most wrong
  If it be His sweet will.

Chapter 12
Of Knowing God's Will

"And [Ananias] said, The God of our fathers hath chosen thee, that thou shouldest know his will, and see that Just One, and shouldest hear the voice of his mouth. For thou shalt be his witness unto all men of what thou hast seen and heard."
—Acts 22:14–15

When Saul said, *"Lord, what wilt thou have me to do?"* (Acts 9:6), he was referring to his personal and immediate duty. When Ananias spoke of his call from God "to know His will," his thought was a much greater one. Saul had been prepared by God as His chosen vessel, to whom He could intrust *"the mystery of his will,"* (Ephesians 1:9) *"the mystery of Christ,"* (verse 9) *"which from the beginning of the world hath been hid in God,"* (Ephesians

3:6) *"that the Gentiles should be fellowheirs, and of the same body and partakers of his promise in Christ by the gospel"* (verse 9).

I have previously spoken about not confining our knowledge of God's will to the commands and promises that have special reference to ourselves. All God's children are called to enlarge their hearts, to take a personal interest in the great work God is seeking to carry out in the world, and so to be ready to take their part in the fulfillment of His purpose. We are all to help in the winning back of the world to Him so that it may be the kingdom of His Son.

In studying Paul's surrender to Christ's will in conversion, we saw how closely it was linked to his vision of the Lord in heaven. Here we find the same connection: Chosen to know His will *and* to see the Just One. The mystery of God's will is the mystery of Christ. To know the will is inseparable from knowing the Just One, who put away sin and is to rule in righteousness on the earth. In the life and writings of Paul, we see how firmly he held the two truths together. It was always Jesus Christ our Lord *"by whom we have received grace and apostleship, for obedience to the faith among all nations, for his name"* (Romans 1:5).

As one who had seen and heard him, Paul's gospel was always a personal witness.

He never preached the will of God as a doctrine, a decree, or even as a revelation without preaching the living person of that Lord Jesus. In Him, God's will revealed all its riches and blessings, and in personal contact with Him alone can its salvation be realized. To know the will and to see the Just One—let these be ever inseparable. The living Christ Himself can alone prepare us to know and do the will of God. To know the will and not see the Just One would make it a new law of Moses—a heavy burden to bear. To see Him is to know the will in the light of God's love, to know it in its divine beauty and perfection, and to receive the power to do it.

All that God did in Paul was *"for a pattern to them which should hereafter believe"* (1 Timothy 1:16). Like him, and through him, each of us is called, in our measure, to know this larger will of God. His purpose for all men is that the Gospel be preached to every person. There is no sadder proof of how little it is understood or preached than the lack, in the majority of Christians, of enthusiastic devotion to the cause of missions. Just as Christ was only in the world to carry out the Father's divine will, so too the church is here for that purpose.

Even among those who do give a measure of support to mission work, there is little sense of the overwhelming prominence that ought to be given to this will of God. It is not one command among others. It is the one thing in which the will of the Father includes everything: that all men would know and honor Christ. It is the one thing for which Christ died and lives. It is the one thing for which the church exists—to be a light to those who are in darkness. It is the one way that a child of God can prove that he lives not unto himself but unto Him who died for him and rose again. It is the one truth that, above all else, needs to be restored to its place. It is the one truth that will assuredly bring about the revival of every other truth of the spiritual life. This is the very will of God, that the church as the body of Christ—and every believer as its member—seek first, absolutely first, the kingdom of God. All are to labor that His will be done throughout the earth, as in heaven.

And why has the church so little understood or fulfilled this will of God? If Paul was divinely enlightened to know that will and to make it known to the church, why has it so little possessed the church of Christ? The answer is not far to seek. Just as in Paul this will of God needed a very special spiritual revelation, it is so still. It is easy, once a truth has been seen and pointed out by spiritual men, for other Christians to see and accept it too. And yet it may be a matter of mental belief, which does not really, through living faith, master and possess the heart. The will of God is a living, spiritual energy. We do not truly know that will until it has entered into and filled our will. As love alone can meet love, and heart alone touch heart, so will alone can grasp will. Anything less is merely a mental image—a conception of the truth, not the thing itself in its reality and power. And so a great deal of the missionary interest of our day proves that the knowledge of this mystery of God's will is not held in the power of the Spirit. Notice the feeble hold it has, the little sacrifice made for it, and the continual bickering over petty details.

Paul spoke of *"the riches of the glory of this mystery among the Gentiles; which is Christ in you, the hope of glory"* (Colossians 1:27). It is only as the mystery of Christ in us—the experience of an indwelling Christ—is truly known that the glory of the mystery will be seen to be this: It is the will of God for all people. The more truly I know, by the Spirit, what it is to have Christ in me, the more I will long and labor that Christ may be in all.

"God...hath chosen thee, that thou shouldest know his will, and see that Just One, and shouldest hear the voice of his mouth. For thou shalt be his witness unto all men of what thou hast seen and heard" (Acts 22:14–15). God gave Paul as an example. In some way, this

word is for you too, my reader. Do believe that the glory of God, Christ, the church, and of every believer is centered in this mystery of God's will for the Gentiles. All God's wisdom, power, holiness, love, and faithfulness meet there. And you are chosen—what a privilege—to know His will and to have it possess you and to use you as its instrument, messenger, and witness.

Do not fear to utterly yield yourself to it, a living sacrifice. *"God...hath chosen thee, that thou shouldest know his will, and* [here is your strength] *see that Just One."* He Himself brought about that will and now works mightily in all who see and receive Him as their Lord who dwells in them. Cast yourself into this mighty stream of divine love—the will of God for the salvation of the ends of the earth. Look up and see and worship the Just One, the Lord our Righteousness, the King of Righteousness, whose rule is to bring peace and blessing to the world. Seek to do all God's will for the establishment of the kingdom. Let it become your one ambition.

Chapter 13
Knowing and Not Doing

"Behold, thou art called a Jew, and restest in the law, and makest thy boast of God, and knowest his will, and approvest the things that are more excellent, being instructed out of the law; and art confident that thou thyself art a guide of the blind, a light of them which are in darkness, an instructor of the foolish, a teacher of babes, which hast the form of knowledge and of the truth in the law. Thou therefore which teachest another, teachest thou not thyself? thou that preachest a man should not steal, dost thou steal?"
—Romans 2:17–21

Chapter one of the epistle to the Romans portrays the terrible unrighteousness of the heathen, with its consequent darkness. Chapter two shows the self-righteousness of the Jews, with the fatal delusion that results from knowing God's will without doing it. Men gloried in God and made their boast of Israel's having had a divine revelation—being the depository of God's will. And yet they never thought about the folly of not doing that will. Christ warned against this same evil when He said, *"Not every one that saith unto me, Lord, Lord, shall enter into the kingdom of heaven; but he that doeth the will of my Father which is in heaven"* (Matthew 7:21).

Today's topic is the terrible possibility of glorying in God, delighting in the study and the knowledge of His will, and yet *not doing it.* Let us try to discover the cause of this sad phenomenon, which is as frequent in the Christian church as it was in Israel. That will surely lead us to its cure. Let us bring our own life into the full light of the teaching of Scripture. Let us find out whether the doing of God's will really has that supreme place in our thought and conduct that it has in the mind of God and the teaching of Christ.

One would think that every Christian would naturally know that doing God's will is the very essence of true faith. Whether we regard Him as Creator, Lawgiver, Father, or Redeemer, we must admit that we cannot honor, please, or fulfill our relationship to Him without living to do His will. Whether we think of the escape from the power of sin, the walk in His fellowship and love, or the participation

in the happiness of His service—here or hereafter—everything points to the doing of God's
will as the only possible way of really living in
the enjoyment of salvation. Why do so many
Christians never know that doing God's will is
the very first duty of the Christian's life, indispensable to its health and safety?

With many, the reason is that they entirely
misunderstand the nature of salvation. They
have misunderstood God's glorious Gospel.
They heard that God justifies the ungodly
freely, by His divine grace. They heard that
they did not have to do or to have done any
works of righteousness to secure God's favor.
They heard right. But they understood wrong.
They were content to believe in the pardon
of sin and deliverance from punishment. Yet
they never saw that salvation means restora-
tion to the love and fellowship of God, to the
honor and blessedness of a walk in obedience
to His will.

Content with being saved from guilt, they
never thought that being saved from the doing
of sin is the real proof of the power of salvation. This is the real entrance into a life in
the likeness and holiness of God. The entire
reasonableness, the unspeakable blessedness,
the indispensable necessity, and the supreme
obligation of seeking and loving to do God's
will as it is done in heaven never dawned on
them. To give up their own wills entirely in

order to follow and carry out God's will never became an article of their creed. They were content with the traditional, conventional view of Christian duty. But they never thought that all that is known of God's will must at once be done.

With others, the cause of failure in doing God's will is a misunderstanding as to the power of salvation. They believe that God's law is unchangeable in its demands and that it is their solemn duty to obey it perfectly. They have learned, from Scripture and experience, how utterly unable they are to fulfill its claims. They have never understood how, in the New Testament, the law of God with its firm demand and condemnation becomes transformed into the will of God. This will does not involve mere demand, but rather actual, living power.

They do not know what it means: You are not under the law, with its impotence, but under grace, with its omnipotence, working in you all that it asks. They are held in bondage of the legal spirit, and they do not believe that it is possible to live a life in the will of God. They admire a promise such as *"My grace is sufficient for thee: for my strength is made perfect in weakness"* (2 Corinthians 12:9). And they delight in a testimony *"I can do all things through Christ which strengtheneth me"* (Philippians 4:13). But they do not dare to expect the fulfillment of either in their own experience. They do not think it is possible to always be doing God's will.

There are still others who believe in both the obligation and the possibility of constantly doing His will and yet complain of continual failure. The reason is that they very often misunderstand their knowledge of God's will. They study God's Word very earnestly to find out God's will, and yet they fail to find the strength to perform it within that knowledge. They do not know that it is only where the light of the Holy Spirit shows God's will that His strength will work it in us.

The will of God, discovered and accepted by our human wisdom, must be obeyed by our human strength. The humble, childlike spirit that believes that the Father will show us what He wants us to do will also receive grace to believe that, for what the Father wants and shows, He will give the needed strength. This He does by His Spirit. It is not enough for us to have the Word and to take out and apply what we think we ought to do. We must wait on God for guidance, to know what He would have us to do. Then, we will learn that to be taught God's will by His Spirit is half the secret of being strengthened by Him to do it.

Believer, Jesus Christ your Savior came to do the will of God and to enable you to do it too! Do you know Him as your Lord who claims to have your whole being, with every power and every moment? Have you acknowledged His lordship and yielded yourself wholly to live only as He would have you? Have you, in the faith of His strength, made this surrender and believed that by His Holy Spirit He seals and maintains it? Then do not be afraid to believe that He will show you all God's will for you and shall prepare you for doing it. Believe that, morning by morning, He will open your ears to hear His voice. To the meek and lowly of heart, He will give God's light and God's strength for all God's will.

Chapter 14

The Renewed Mind Proving God's Will

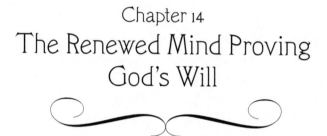

"Be not conformed to this world: but be ye transformed by the renewing of your mind, that ye may prove what is that good, and acceptable, and perfect, will of God."
—Romans 12:2

The twelfth chapter of Romans begins with Paul imploring believers to present their bodies as a living sacrifice, holy and acceptable to God. In verse two, he called these God-devoted men, if their sacrifice was indeed to be acceptable to God, to prove—to find out and show—what the acceptable will of God actually is. He who wants to live as an acceptable sacrifice must live in the acceptable will of God. The one acceptable sacrifice is the doing of the acceptable will. To live in the will of God is the only thing that can make us well-pleasing to Him. The one and only object and proof of true consecration is doing the will of God.

The three adjectives Paul used—*"good,"* *"acceptable,"* and *"perfect"*—indicate three stages in our proving and knowing the will of God. The first refers to our discerning between good and evil, and our accepting what we know of God's will as indeed good. The second points to our knowledge of God's will in special relation to ourselves. The will of God is not the same for all His children. As we discover what the will of God is for ourselves, we know that what we do is actually acceptable and well-pleasing to Him. The third word, *"perfect,"* tells us that we may not rest content with what we already know and do of God's will. This is only a beginning; we must press on to stand perfect in all the will of God.

To know and accept the will of God as good is the first step, and it is good. To know it in our personal relationship to Him as well-pleasing is better. To know the perfect will of God is best of all. It is the true aim of the full, Christian life. So we can prove and know for ourselves, so we can prove to men, what is the good, acceptable, and perfect will of God. So we yield our bodies as an acceptable sacrifice. The first great call of this epistle—Live wholly as sacrifices to God—is followed, at once, by its complement—Live only to do the will of God (Romans 12:1–2).

A warning and an exhortation are inserted between these two commands: *"Be not conformed to this world"* is the warning that reveals our first and greatest danger. *"Be ye transformed by the renewing of your mind"* is the exhortation that reveals the path and the strength in which it becomes possible to overcome the danger and stand perfect in all the will of God.

If you indeed want to know and do God's will, listen to the warning, *"Be not conformed to this world." "The friendship of the world is enmity with God"* (James 4:4). Its major downfall—by which it became a *"world that lieth in wickedness"* (1 John 5:19)—was the rejection of the will of God. The world may acknowledge a God, but it cannot and will not do His will. It cannot, by its very nature, do anything but its own will. We are, by nature, of the world. We are still in it and in constant danger of being under its influence.

After our regeneration, the secret, subtle atmosphere with which the world surrounds us, and with which the flesh is in alliance, hinders thousands of Christians from seeking a life of true and full devotion to the will of God. Unless we reject its principles, its pleasures, and its pursuits with our whole heart, we will gradually lose the spiritual capacity for delighting in and performing God's will. Unless we come out from the world—where self-will and self-pleasing rule—we can never live the life in which the believer seeks only to be a sacrifice well-pleasing to God—to prove the well-pleasing will of God. Do let us believe it—the great cause of failure in doing the will of God is simply a worldly spirit. Therefore, beware: *"Be not conformed to this world."*

The negative, not being conformed to the world, must be accompanied by the positive: *"But be ye transformed by the renewing of your mind."* The renewal in regeneration, once and for all, must be followed up by the continual, daily, renewing of the Holy Spirit. *"Be renewed in the spirit of your mind"* (Ephesians 4:23). *"He saved us, by the washing of regeneration, and renewing of the Holy Ghost"* (Titus 3:5). This is the only power that can enable us to be living, holy, and acceptable sacrifices. It is the only way that we can be truly prepared to delight in doing the will of God. Attempting to do the will of God with a heart that does not daily seek and find the renewing of the Holy Spirit in the spirit of the mind, will end in failure. Only a healthy man can do a healthy man's work. Only a spiritual man can walk in the spiritual path of obedience to all God's will.

I ask you, beloved believer, to pause and think about the lessons we have been taught. The calling and the privilege of every believer is to find out what the good and acceptable will of God is. It is impossible to fulfill this calling without definitely yielding ourselves to live as holy sacrifices, well-pleasing to God in everything. The one great hindrance to this is a worldly spirit that conforms to the dispositions and habits of the world. The only power that can overcome this danger is that of the Holy Spirit. To be daily "transformed in the renewing of our minds" gives the spiritual capacity to know, to love, and to do all God's will.

If you find that you are not yet living this life, do not rest until you know and possess it. If it is because you have never definitely and finally accepted God's will as your life, oh, do so now! If it is because you have never presented yourself a living sacrifice—come at once, and yield to God's claim! By the mercies of God, I beseech you: Give up yourself to the God who redeemed you. If you have done so but still fail because you did not know there was so much of the world in you—begin at once to live the life of not being conformed to the world. Be transformed by the renewing of the Holy Spirit.

Take courage, my brethren! The eternal Spirit, through whom Christ said, *"I delight to do thy will"* (Psalm 40:8) and offered Himself a sacrifice unto God, dwells in you. Yield yourselves as a sacrifice for Him to consume. Believe and receive His daily renewing. He will prepare you for proving all the perfect will of God.

Chapter 15
According to the Will of God

*"Our Lord Jesus Christ, who gave himself for
our sins, that he might deliver us from this
present evil world, according to the will of God
and our Father."*
—Galatians 1:3–4

P aul always carried with him a very deep
sense of the will of God as the source and
the rule of all things. In five of the Epistles, he
spoke of himself as an apostle, *"by the will of
God"* (2 Corinthians 1:1). The thought of God's
will dominated his whole ministry—inspiring
at once devotion, obedience, and perfect confidence. He loved to think of God's will working
out its purpose through him. Of his intention
to visit Rome, he spoke more than once as
coming to them *"by the will of God."* (See, for
example, Romans 1:10.) Of the Macedonians
giving themselves first to the Lord and then

to him, he said too, that it was *"by the will of God"* (2 Corinthians 8:5).

And so here, in speaking of the work of God's Son in our redemption, he showed how its chief characteristic is that it was *"according to the will of God."* Whether in his own life, in the grace manifested in his converts, or in the work of our Lord Jesus, salvation was to him the will of God manifesting itself and working out His purpose.

The expression he uses in regard to Christ's work is a somewhat unusual and remarkable one. *"Who gave himself for our sins, that he might deliver us from this present evil world, according to the will of God and our Father."* It gives us a new aspect of the Father's will as revealed in Christ's death. In our last meditation (Romans 12:2) we saw how, in the spiritual life, being conformed to the world was the first great danger of the consecrated soul. And we saw how being transformed out of it into the newness of life is the only way to a life in the good and perfect will of God.

Here, we discover the deepest root of that teaching. The whole will of God in Christ's death had this one object—to deliver us from this present, evil world. The spirit of the world and the will of God are directly opposed to one another. The will of God demands and promises and works entire deliverance from it. If we want to know the will of God correctly and live according to it, we must be entirely separate from all that is of this present, evil world. That alone is true and full salvation.

"This present evil world." And was not this world created by God? And is it all so entirely evil as to deserve the name "this evil world" and to need the Son of God to deliver us from it? Yes. Scripture teaches that with the entrance of sin into the world it came into the power of the prince of evil. When, in Adam's fall, Satan obtained power over him, the world, over which he was to have been king, fell with him. Satan became the god of this world, and all men are born into it. The world is now an organized kingdom of evil, ruled by the god and enlivened by the spirit of the world. *"The whole world lieth in wickedness"* (1 John 5:19).

The development of evil, in its slow growth as well as its sudden outbreaks, is no blind evolution. It is the result of a deliberate, systematic war of an intelligent power of evil against the rule of God. Whether in the grossest forms of heathenism, amid the refinement of art and culture, or even under the guise of a nominal Christianity—the world lies in darkness everywhere. In its principles and aims, it is the very opposite of the kingdom of God and of heaven. Its distinguishing characteristics are the pursuit of the visible, the assertion of man's will against that of God, and the pride of man's wisdom. They are in contrast with the will, the love, and the service of the invisible God.

Jesus Christ came to deliver us out of this present, evil world by freeing us from its spirit and making us partakers of the life and the powers of the heavenly world. In His discourse with rulers of this world, both among the Jews and before Pilate, He often expressed the truth, "Ye are of this world; I am from above. I am not of this world; My kingdom is not of this world." (See, for example, John 8:23). He also claimed this "otherworldliness" for His disciples: *"Ye are not of the world, but I have chosen you out of the world, therefore the world hateth you"* (John 15:19).

He described His work as an overcoming of the world and a casting out of the prince of the world. He encouraged His disciples to expect and, in the power of His victory, to endure the enmity of the world. The life He brought with Him from heaven and came to impart to us was very different from that of the world. Yes, more so even than heaven is higher than earth. The great object of His work was to deliver us from this present, evil world, according to the will of God.

This is an aspect of truth that barely enters into the preaching or the practice of our days. We sometimes hear of a worldly Christianity and of a believing world, but there appears to be little awareness of the extent to which a worldly spirit pervades and weakens the Christian life. We are all born and bred under the power of the spirit of the world. It is so difficult to exactly define or recognize its power and influence. We are so little warned of the need of our entire deliverance from that spirit by the Spirit of God dispelling it and taking its place that one often sees an earnest and active Christian life with little of the truly unworldly and heavenly spirit. As a consequence of this, the power of Jesus Christ, of faith in Him, of overcoming the world, and of proving that we are just as little of the world as He was, is little sought or known.

Our Lord *"gave himself...that he might deliver us from this present evil world, according to the will of God."* Is it any wonder that His full revelation in the heart is so little enjoyed? Only he who seeks to have Jesus do His perfect work is ready for complete separation, and he who desires emancipation from the spirit of the world can expect it.

Let each one of us who wants to prove, know, and do the perfect will of God study the lesson: God wills complete deliverance from this present, evil world. To this end, Jesus Christ gave Himself for us. As we receive Him to live in us, that will shall be done in us. We are surrounded on every side by the powers of the spirit of this world. We are unable to resist, or even to recognize them, unless they are revealed to us by the Spirit of God. Without our even being aware of it, the spirit of the world is present in the literature and newspapers of the day, the interest and attraction of politics and commerce, and in culture and entertainment. In our own hearts, the love of self with its honor and pleasure, the desire of and dependence on the visible, and the lack of absolute surrender to God and His will are all signs of a worldly spirit. Not until we allow the Spirit of God to convict us of all this, and to possess us with all that is its opposite, can we fully know the deliverance that Christ gives according to the will of God.

May God help us to inseparably connect the three blessed truths set before us here: the will of God, as the source; Jesus giving Himself for us, as the means; and deliverance from this present, evil world, as the mark and fruit of the great salvation. May He teach us that we are as little of this world as Jesus was, because we are one with Him. And may the presence and power of the Son of God from heaven in our hearts, with its complete deliverance from a worldly spirit, be known as the will of God for us.

Chapter 16
God Working Out His Own Will

"Being predestinated according to the purpose of him who worketh all things after the counsel of his own will."
—Ephesians 1:11

In the epistle to the Ephesians, we have three passages concerning the will of God. Chapter one points us back to the eternal mystery of that will in God and tells us how, as God purposed, He Himself works it all out. Chapter five calls us to seek to understand what the will of God is. Chapter six brings us down into practical life and teaches us how the most common drudgery of daily duty may be done as the will of God. As in the heights of heaven and eternity, the will of God claims supreme authority over the conduct and heart of the humblest Christian. Let us begin to study it in its origin and work before the foundation of the world.

Paul wrote of God having:

Predestinated us unto the adoption of children by Jesus Christ to himself, according to the good pleasure of his will...according to the riches of his grace; wherein he hath abounded toward us...having made known unto us the mystery of his will, according to his good pleasure which he hath purposed in himself...in whom also we have obtained an inheritance, being predestinated according to the purpose of him who worketh all things after the counsel of his own will. (Ephesians 1:5, 7–9, 11)

Each expression has its significance. The *"good pleasure of his will"* means the absolute liberty of God. It is the perfection of the will that knows no higher reason than that it so pleased Him.

The predestination, election, and foreordaining of God's children had their origin in Him. *"The mystery of his will"* suggests that it was hidden in God. We can only know as much of it as He reveals, and even what He reveals is still beyond our comprehension. *"The purpose"* of His will refers to the great plan or scheme to be carried out that His holy will formed for itself. And *"the counsel"* of His will reminds us of the divine *"wisdom and prudence"* (verse 8) holding counsel with itself. It is the ordering of all things so as to prove that His good pleasure is indeed all that is most right and good and perfect. The salvation of His church, and of every member of it, lies hidden in the secret depths of God's will and its predestining purpose.

"Being predestinated according to the purpose of him who worketh all things after the counsel of his own will." What God has willed, He also works out. The counsel of His will is too high and holy; only He can work it out. The will is a working power, a determination to act. Even a man who really wills a thing seeks to overcome every obstacle so that it may be realized. We need, as we study and worship the will of God, to give full attention to the conviction that God Himself works out all things after the counsel of His will. The eternal purpose is what guides all His work. All that the eternal purpose determined must and will be brought about by Him. This faith will teach us some very precious lessons.

It inspires the assurance that God's purpose will be performed. We are so apt to look to ourselves and our feebleness, to men and to circumstances, and to measure what appears possible by these. We need to remember that God's sovereign will is a power that shall—in great and small detail—infallibly secure the fulfillment of His plans. In our own hearts and lives, and in the service of His kingdom in which we take part, we need to definitely know Him as the *"God which worketh all in all"* (1 Corinthians 12:6). We speak of man's relationship to God as that of cooperation. But divine operation always precedes human cooperation. Unceasing and continuous, divine operation draws forth and inspires human cooperation. All feebleness in the divine life and all failure in spiritual work is due to this one thing: We do not make room for and wait on the divine operation. We seek to do the divine will without the living faith in Him who Himself works all things after the counsel of His will.

This faith will teach us to live and work in entire dependence on God's working. It will awaken and strengthen us in humility, the root of all true, Christian virtue. It is through this that the angels keep their first estate—they live in entire dependence on God's willing and working in them. It was for this that the Son assumed the robe of manhood. He came to teach us that the life and glory of man consists of continually receiving what we are to be, to will, or to do from God. He did nothing of Himself but what the Father showed Him. He judged nothing of Himself, but as He heard, so He spoke. The connection between God and ourselves is to be one of unending receptivity. God will constantly impart the life and strength we need. As we learn to know God thus, we will fear nothing so much as hindering His work by our own, and—under the guise of doing His will—making it impossible for Him to do His will. Oh, let us, in deep humility and reverence, worship and wait on the God who works all things after the counsel of His own will.

This faith will lead us to true diligence in God's service in the blessed confidence of being able to do all His will, because what He wills He works Himself. At first sight, it appears as if this entire, unceasing dependence on God might hinder us in our work. That is true only as long as we do not fully understand or believe it. But to the upright, who wait on God, the light of understanding will emerge. The same applies to this as to the truth of faith without works for obtaining justification. At first, it appears as if this would discourage good works in the believer. But as we indeed give ourselves away to the blessed truth of faith without works for acceptance, we find that it is this very faith that is most abundant in producing good works as its fruit.

Even so, as we fully accept the truth of which we were at first afraid—that we can do nothing of ourselves and that God must do all—we will experience that the most absolute and unceasing dependence is the secret of the most effective service. Works before faith only hinder and the attempt to work without the fullest and most entire dependence on God leads to continual failure. We must cease living entirely for ourselves and our works, yield ourselves unreservedly to God's working, and there learn what it means to say, *"I also labour, striving according to his working, which worketh in me mightily"* (Colossians 1:29). The faith of our entire weakness and dependence upon God becomes the power for our highest activity.

"Predestinated according to the purpose of him who worketh all things after the counsel of his own will." Believer, the purpose according to and for which you have been predestined is that of a God who works all things after the counsel of His will. Let every thought of the will of God be accompanied by the faith that He is a God who Himself works all things that He wills. All goodness and power are His, to be received directly from Him alone through Christ Jesus. Worship Him with a holy fear, so that you don't grieve your Lord by your much serving, like Martha. Instead, be like Mary; wait for what He can work in you. What God has joined together, let no man put asunder— God works His will in man by the Holy Spirit, and man works out the will of God, worked in him secretly, in his daily life and duty.

Chapter 17
Understanding the Will of God

*"Be ye not unwise, but understanding what
the will of the Lord is."*
—Ephesians 5:17

In the preceding chapter, I spoke of the three passages in this epistle that refer to the will of God. The first lifted us up into the eternal glory to worship God. His will is the revelation of His glory, and He Himself works it out in time. The last of these three lessons will lead us to the burden of the slave and show us how even there, in the most commonplace, everyday life, the will of God may be done on earth as in heaven. Our present subject stands between the two as the indispensable link. It is only as I know the will of God— both in the place it has in His life and in mine—that I can appreciate the blessedness and fulfill the duty of only doing the will of the Father. The danger of neglecting the careful study necessary to know all that God's will implies made Paul write, *"Be ye not unwise, but understanding what the will of the Lord is."*

"Be ye not unwise." With our pride in our Christian education, common sense, and daily Bible reading, we think that we know well enough what God's will must be. In assuming so, we prove that we are as fools, without the wisdom of God guiding us.

> Let no man deceive himself. If any man among you seemeth to be wise in this world, let him become a fool, that he may be wise....If any man think that he knoweth any thing, he knoweth nothing yet as he ought to know. (1 Corinthians 3:18; 8:2)

Let us beware of the folly of thinking that we know the will of God. Let us become fools indeed, in the sense of our great ignorance, and wisely seek the divine teaching that alone can correctly reveal the divine will.

"Be ye not unwise, but understanding what the will of the Lord is." To understand a thing means not only to know its outward form, but also to know something of its true nature—its inner meaning and working. It is only as the believer seeks spiritual insight into God's will that the doing of it will become the heavenly

joy it is meant to be. Let us consider what some of the main elements of the true understanding of God's will are.

Think of it, first of all, in connection with God Himself. His will is the power by which He determines what He is to do and what is to be done by His children. In that will, all His goodness, wisdom, love, and power are revealed. The knowledge of that will opens up to mankind the very heart of God. In the surrender to and worship of that will, angels and men rise into living fellowship with God. Over the carrying out of that will, God Himself watches. What the divine wisdom has planned, divine power will perform. Never for a moment can the will of God be separated from God Himself. If you want to understand that will, never think of it as anything less than the symbol of the presence of the living God Himself. Always seek to see God in His will.

Think of it, then, as it is made known in His Word. The words of Holy Scripture are, for the most part, plain and simple. They can be understood by all. And yet, because they contain the mystery of divine wisdom, the understanding of the meaning of the words does not at all ensure the real spiritual understanding or grasp of God's will. The words need to be taken into the heart—into the faith and love and obedience of man's whole being. And we need God's divine working through them before we can fully understand God's will. The very same Spirit, which, having searched the deep things of God, inspired the Word, must give His light and life in the depths of our heart too, if the will of God is really to become our will. Without this, all our knowledge is merely intellectual and superficial. Only God working His will into our will, with our will accepting it heartily, can prepare us to understand what the will of the Lord is.

Think of that will especially as it is embodied in Christ Jesus. He is the Word of God, the visible image of the hidden glory of God's will. As man, He came to show us how it is the calling and the blessedness of mankind to give itself up wholly to the will of God. He came to show us that we could do nothing of ourselves and must count most confidently on God Himself working in us both to will and to do all His will. As our Redeemer, He died to deliver us from our own will, and now He leads us in the path of dying to self, to live and do God's will alone. Any attempt to understand the will of God, apart from its intimate union with the Son of God our Savior, ends in foolishness. It is in living union with Jesus alone that either light or strength for knowing and doing the Father's will can come.

Understand what the will of the Lord is. *Think of its claim on your whole life.* You cannot attempt to fully yield to or rejoice in that claim until you see that it rests in the New Testament promises. The renewed will is a ray of the divine will itself, taking possession of you—of your inner being—and from within, enabling you to love God's will as wholly and as naturally as you formerly loved your self-will. The three-in-one God has begun His own life in you. His will and the power that works it out are in you; in the faith of that heartily admit the claim of God's will to have complete dominion. See, and say, that there is to be nothing in your life that is not under the control, or rather, the inspiration of God's will.

With faith in this living root of God's will possessing you, look on the Word with its exceeding breadth covering every possible position and on your daily life with its innumerable needs and duties, and then understand how the will of God can be carried out through all. Your will and His will shall be inseparably intertwined. *"Created in Christ Jesus unto good works, which God hath before ordained that we should walk in them"* (Ephesians 2:10). You can count on the Holy Spirit to lead you into all of God's perfect will.

Understand what the will of the Lord is. To sum up all, think of God's will as more than having come forth from an infinite love—revealed and embodied in the written and the eternal Word and claiming your whole life down to the minutest of details. Above all, think of it as the promise of what God Himself will work in you. Understand that the will of God is so divine, holy, and perfect that only God Himself can work it. You can only work it as He works it in you by His Holy Spirit.

The stronger and more unceasing and more joyfully confident your faith in God's working all His will in you becomes, the more you will know that it is possible for you to do that will. *"According to your faith be it unto you"* (Matthew 9:29) will again be made true in you. Standing in the full light of the eternal love as it shines on you from heaven, you will find that that light shines on the whole of the Word and of life. And you will then begin to understand what the will of the Lord is. It is the most wonderful, beautiful, blessed thing in the universe. It is the one thing to be sought and loved, to be done or suffered. It is the one thing worth living and dying for.

Chapter 18
Doing from the Heart

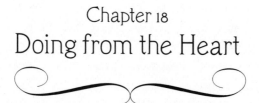

"Servants, be obedient to them that are your masters according to the flesh, with fear and trembling, in singleness of your heart, as unto Christ; not with eyeservice, as menpleasers; but as the servants of Christ, doing the will of God from the heart; with good will doing service, as to the Lord, and not to men."
—Ephesians 6:5–7

The importance of the teaching these words contain can hardly be overrated. They teach that when we are fulfilling some direct command as well as when we are doing our common, daily work, all is and may be done as the will of God. This cannot be done except as it is done—*"in singleness of heart...from the heart"*—with the joyful and loving consent of our whole being. The strength to thus act is found in doing all in Christ's presence, unto Him. They teach us too, how the most common, daily life, with its drudgery, or even its oppression, may be transfigured into the work of heaven—doing the will of God.

The passage derives special force from the fact that it was addressed to slaves. At that time, almost all servants were slaves. They were at the disposal of their masters and had no legal rights. Many of the early Christians were slaves. Their servitude was often harsh and thankless. The very liberty and brotherhood that the Gospel preached only made some of them even more aware of the bondage they endured. To such, Paul wrote to be obedient to their masters, as unto Christ, and to perform all their service as the will of God from the heart. If this was expected of these slaves, how much more should we learn the lesson that everything we do, even the compulsory or ill-requited service of a hard master, is to be done as the will of God?

And how can this disposition be attained? Only in one way: by heartily accepting any situation we encounter as God's will for us. Then, the work we have to do in that situation will be God's will for us. In our opening chapter, we saw that one of the first lessons in the Christian life is to accept every trouble that comes to us from the mistakes of ourselves or others or the trial of circumstances as God's appointment. His providence is His will for us.

This alone can prevent the irritation, anger, and worry that so often embitters life and clouds the sense of God's favor. Then, nothing under heaven can disturb our faith or peace. To see God in all gives rest and hope.

Every work we have to perform, however unpleasant, unjust, or ill-rewarded, becomes, as long as God allows it, His will for us. To do it as such makes it easy and holy—a well-pleasing sacrifice. And if this is true of the slave's work, it is even more true of all the duties of our daily lives. In housekeeping, business, and the multitude of work involved in earning a living or fulfilling a calling, everything must be done as the will of God.

Almost immediately, this thought of all work being done as God's will seems to be out of our reach. Who always remembers—with so much to occupy and disturb—that this common work is all God's will? There is only one way to succeed in doing this, and that is to do the work *"in singleness of your heart,"* *"from the heart."* The heart means desire, will, love, delight, and joy. What we do from the heart is a pleasure. The only faith that satisfies God is that of the heart. That is why He asks us to love Him with the whole heart. As long as we only take God's will as a law that we are obliged to obey for our own safety and happiness, or to prove our faith and gratitude, the doing of it is a burden. But when we take it into our hearts as a thing we delight in and cannot have too much of—what we have given up our life for—everything that gives us an opportunity to do more of that blessed will, and to keep our devotion to it unbroken, is welcome.

"Doing the will of God from the heart." God not only asks for the heart; He has also promised to put His law into our heart. God wants the hearts, and nothing less can please Him. Therefore, He has made provision for securing it. He sends forth the Spirit of His Son into our hearts. Let us believe in the Holy Spirit dwelling in us and imparting the love of God. Let us, in that faith, worship and give ourselves away to the beautiful, sweet will of God, and cherish it as our choicest treasure and chief desire. As it gets possession of the heart and opens itself in it, the heart that has learned to adore its glory in God will also learn to welcome every trace of it on earth. We will find ourselves doing the hardest service in singleness of heart, with the heart set only on pleasing God—in very deed doing the will of God from the heart. Our text tells us one thing more—how doing the will of God will always be connected with the presence of Christ. The will of God and the Son of God are inseparable. Jesus is the will of God. He did it. He works that will from heaven. His great work as Savior is to secure our doing it. And, so, Paul wrote to the slaves,

Be obedient to them that are your masters...as unto Christ...Not with eyeservice, as menpleasers; but as the servants of Christ, doing the will of God from the heart; with good will doing service, as to the Lord. (Ephesians 6:5–9)

The fact that the motivating force is that we do it as a service rendered to the Lord we love is repeated three times. His presence and His pleasure are to be our inspiration. The poor slave could understand that. The fear of displeasing his master spurred him on to continuous effort.

The presence of Jesus Christ, the sense of being His servant, and the glory of pleasing Him can unceasingly fill your heart and carry you throughout the day, doing work for men as His servant. The presence of Christ prepares us for this. He knows what difficulties and temptations are in the way of always doing God's will. He knows how the victory can be obtained, and the will of God always be done. He lives to secure for us the strength and the victory.

If we live to be nothing less than wholly His servants in ever doing God's will alone—if we trust Him to maintain His own presence in us all the day—we can know the joy of His service in His strength.

"Doing the will of God from the heart." Let God, let Jesus Christ, God's Son, let God's

love, have the heart, the whole heart, and nothing less. And, then, God's will shall be done by us on earth as it is in heaven. God Himself will work it in us. And amid all the changing circumstances of life, there will be one thing that never changes—our place of rest in the center of God's will.

Chapter 19

Filled with the Knowledge of God's Will

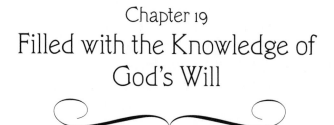

"Epaphras, who is one of you, a servant of Christ, saluteth you, always labouring fervently for you in prayers, that ye may stand perfect and complete in all the will of God."
—Colossians 4:12

In the first chapter of the epistle, we had Paul praying. Here, we have Epaphras. The prayers of both refer to this one thing—the supreme importance of the will of God in the Christian life. Paul had prayed that their hearts might be filled with the spiritual knowledge of God's will. Then, they would walk worthy of the Lord and be all pleasing. Epaphras prayed that their lives might be so filled with that will that they would *"stand perfect and complete in all the will of God."*

Paul said that he did not cease to pray thus. (See Colossians 1:9.) Of Epaphras, he said that he always labors for them in his prayers. In both cases, the relation to God's will is to be no partial or divided one, but rather whole and entire, as expressed by the word *all*. Paul asked that they might be filled with the knowledge of His will in *all* wisdom, to walk worthy of the Lord unto *all* pleasing. Epaphras labored for them in his prayers that they might stand complete in *all* the will of God. Nothing less than *all God's will* is to be the standard, the desire, the prayer, and the hope of the believer.

"Stand perfect and complete in all the will of God" is the believer's only standard. How can it be otherwise? The will of God is one whole—equally divine, beautiful, and blessed. All are of equal obligation, equally necessary for our peace and perfection. And equal provision is made for its performance in the grace that is in Christ Jesus. The will of God is so entirely one with the nature, perfection, and love of God that to neglect or refuse any part of it makes it impossible for God to fully reveal Himself to us and to bless us. The believer's acceptance of and surrender to God's will as his only standard should be as perfect and complete as it is as a whole.

Paul and Epaphras regarded this as an attainable measure of perfection among the

Colossians. Many Christians admit that the words express God's standard of duty, but they rob that admission of all its power by believing it to be impossible. They think that the standard is only an ideal one, not really practicable or practical. They often regard it as the law of Moses, with its demands that can never be fulfilled.

They do not understand the words in Romans 6:14, *"Ye are not under the law"*—a law that demands what you cannot do and gives no power to do. We can now live *"under grace"*—a grace that demands only what it will give and work in us and so enables us to do all it demands. All His will is God's standard for us, and it is actually provided for. Let it be our standard too. Your Father asks nothing less; let nothing less be what you ask of Him and offer to Him.

To *"stand perfect and complete in all the will of God"* is the believer's one desire. Desire is the one great power in the world that urges and enables men to undertake and accomplish what at first appears to be impossible. When a man has his heart set on something, difficulties only awaken his energy and increase his power to attain it. Oh, that Christians might be taught and trained to set their heart on *"all the will of God"* as their highest and only blessedness. May they desire to *"stand perfect"* in it as the one hope of their calling!

It is possible that the preaching of the will of God has not had the same place as the preaching of the grace of God. Men have not seen that grace is nothing but the will of God manifested. And as grace came through Christ's doing of that will, so its one object is to unite us with that will and have it done in us as it is done in heaven. Doing the will of God has been something additional—a supplement to what the grace of God has done, an expression of gratitude—instead of being the very door into all the love, salvation, and blessedness out of which the grace came and into which it leads. If we understood this, every desire for help from God for salvation, happiness, and the enjoyment of His love would be identified with standing perfect and complete in all that will. It is here that God is revealed and is alone to be found. Let us set our heart on this.

To *"stand perfect and complete in all the will of God"* is the believer's continual prayer. The teaching about the knowledge of God's will, and the standing complete in God's will, are associated with the telling of Paul's unceasing prayer and Epaphras' laboring fervently. It is not earnest thought, clear understanding, or strong desire that will bring us what we need—but unceasing prayer. Doing the will of God is the life of heaven, because God is there. He works His will without hindrance in all the souls who are wholly yielded up to Him and ever wait upon Him.

It is from God in heaven that this heavenly life of doing His will must come down. And it will come down and be carried on and maintained in us in proportion to our waiting on and yielding to God. We must continually offer ourselves up to His Holy Spirit to work in us. Whether it is in the quiet, steady perseverance of our daily prayer, the fervent striving in times when the need and the desire are especially felt, or in the inward supplication of the heart that prays without ceasing, only the life that is continually looking upward will feel that God's standard is not too high. We must solely depend on God's working His own will in us, because what the word of His mouth demands, the power of His hand performs.

To *"stand perfect and complete in all the will of God"* is the believer's sure hope. Paul and Epaphras were praying out of their blessed experience. Unfortunately, we have grown so accustomed to praying for things that we never expect. They lived under the power of the Holy Spirit. They saw so much to grieve and disappoint them, yet they remained faithful. There were some whom they could call spiritual men. And they knew that in answer to their prayer it would be given—men filled with the knowledge of God's will, in all wisdom;

men who could *"stand perfect and complete in all the will of God."*

Let us pray without ceasing. Let us strive always for the churches or the saints with whom we are connected that these two prayers may be fulfilled in them. Let us ask God to reveal in ourselves and our experience the full truth and meaning of these two prayers. Amid all disappointment let us say, "My soul, find hope in God! I will praise Him for the help of His countenance!" Let us set our hope on God, who works all things after the purpose of His will. God must ever be God alone. Heaven and the heavenly nature are His and must be received only from Him. And they must be preserved only by an entire trust in Him.

God alone can work His will in us. In a heart that prays and waits without ceasing in dependence on Him, He can and will do it. Let us believe that these precious words of Epaphras' prayer are not vain. In them, the Holy Spirit reveals the sure hope of every believer who will trust God. Let us not doubt, but rather *"stand perfect and complete in all the will of God."*

Chapter 20

Stand Perfect and Complete

"We...do not cease to pray for you...that ye might be filled with the knowledge of his will in all wisdom and spiritual understanding."
—Colossians 1:9

Understanding the place this prayer should have in the Christian life and realizing how to be *"filled with the knowledge of* [God's] *will in all wisdom"* are the very root of spiritual growth and health. Notice the beautiful description of the walk a believer follows as a result of the blessing this prayer is meant to bring. The result of being filled with the knowledge of God's will is that we will *"walk worthy of the Lord unto all pleasing"* (Colossians 1:10); *"that we bear fruit in every good work"* (verse 10); *"that we increase in the knowledge of God"* (verse 10); that we are *"strengthened with all might, according* to *his glorious power, unto all patience and long-suffering with joyfulness; giving thanks unto the Father"* (Colossians 1:11). All these are the sure portion of a soul *"filled with the knowledge of his will in all wisdom and spiritual understanding."* It is the will of God that all these things would be in us and abound. Where the heart is filled and possessed with the knowledge of all this indeed being God's will, the life will be filled with its fruits.

We have already spoken of the knowledge of God's will. The great truth suggested by these words in regard to it is that it must be in *"all wisdom and spiritual understanding."* There is a wisdom and an understanding of the truths of Scripture that is not spiritual. The human mind can study and grasp the doctrines the Bible teaches concerning God and the divine life in man without having any true insight or knowledge of quickening life and power.

Christians, to a very large extent, study their Bibles, listen to preaching, and read Christian books believing that they earnestly desire to know the truth. And some are able to grasp it, but they do not wait for the real spiritual wisdom and understanding from God to make it their own—to prove its power in their life. They wonder why so much Bible knowledge does not make them humble and lowly as they would like to be. They never know that it is simply because their knowledge of God's will is in the power of human wisdom and natural understanding. And such knowledge is powerless to effectively work what God's Word has promised to work.

In His farewell discourse, our Lord said to His disciples, *"The Holy Ghost...shall teach you all things, and bring all things to your remembrance, whatsoever I have said unto you....The Spirit of truth, is come, he will guide you into all truth"* (John 14:26; 16:13). The power of teaching divine truth and leading men into it was committed to the Holy Spirit alone. He was to teach *all* things, to guide into *all* truth. No truth could be truly known without His teaching. As the indwelling Spirit, who would possess and renew the heart, He alone could impart the truth so that it would become part of our very nature—giving both the will and the power to obey it.

Our Lord taught His disciples many things while He was on earth with them. But they understood very little of what He said. They were able to obey His commands of self-denial, meekness, humility, and love even less. When the Holy Spirit came down from heaven into their hearts as the power of God—the Spirit of His Son—the words of God came to them in their spiritual, supernatural, quickening power.

We need to study this. As no one can worship God in spirit and in truth except through
the Holy Spirit, so no one can have any
spiritual understanding of God's will except
through the Spirit. The one reason that our
knowledge of God's will is so defective in its
extent and power, that we see so little beauty
in God's will, and that we seldom delight or
succeed in fulfilling it is simply this: The
knowledge is not in all wisdom and spiritual
understanding.

And what is needed to get this spiritual
wisdom through the Holy Spirit's teaching?
One great thing—we must be spiritual people.
Paul said to the Corinthians, *"I, brethren could
not speak unto you as unto spiritual, but as
unto carnal"* (1 Corinthians 3:1). They were
unfit for full spiritual teaching because they
were not spiritually minded. This suggests to
us the law of all the Holy Spirit's teaching. He
cannot communicate spiritual truths to those
whose lives are worldly, selfish, or carnal. He
needs a disposition that at least longs to be
spiritual to be able to work. It is in the heart
that He gives His teaching. The man who
yields his life to be led and ruled by Him will
be taught by Him. Such a person can be filled
with the knowledge of God's will.

Notice the word *filled.* It points to an emp-
tying out and putting aside of all else. It suggests a heart given up wholly and entirely to

the will of God. It promises a life in which the will of God spontaneously enters into the minutest details of daily life—the whole heart filled with it and with nothing else. Do not look at it as a multitude of commandments all packed together, but rather as God's grand will—the controlling power of the life, inspiring and animating the whole being. The two thoughts accompany and complement each other—the whole being surrendered to be spiritual and receive spiritual wisdom, and the whole being thus filled with the knowledge of God's will.

For this, Paul did not cease to pray and make requests for the Colossians. Let us pray for God's church and ourselves, that the spiritual filling with the knowledge of God's will may be given to us. The blessing is waiting for us; the Father delights to give it. It is our birthright—a divine birth needs and has the promise of a divine education. The Spirit through whom we received the divine life can alone, and will most surely, guide us to all its riches. Let us pray unceasingly, honestly, believingly, to be filled with the knowledge of God's will *"in all wisdom and spiritual understanding."*

In heaven the will of God is done. Nothing but the heavenly life can do it. No one except God's Spirit can do God's will. Let us not expect to know or do it without the heavenly life working in us by the Spirit come down from heaven into our heart. The heavenly life delights in God's will. This is one of the great lessons that the church needs to learn. The universal neglect of so much of God's will and the universal complaint of the lack of power to perform has but one cause: The heavenly life in the power of the Holy Spirit is so little known or sought.

Brethren, learn the lesson that no knowledge and no book can profit you except as it reminds you of your need for the One and Only Teacher. The Spirit of Truth must lead you in inward adoration and teachableness to wait for the hidden spiritual wisdom that He alone gives.

Chapter 21
Your Sanctification

"For this is the will of God, even your sanctification."
—1 Thessalonians 4:3

The apostle closed the third chapter of this epistle with the wondrous prayer for the Thessalonian believers that the Lord might *"establish their hearts unblameable in holiness before God, even our Father"* (1 Thessalonians 3:13). He proceeded in chapter four to urge them to a walk well-pleasing to God. He began by specially warning them against two sins, uncleanness and fraud (1 Thessalonians 4:3–7). And, then, just as he had pleaded with God to establish them unblameable in holiness, he pleaded with them to remember and yield to the blessed truth: *"This is the will of God, even your sanctification."* *"God hath not called us unto uncleanness, but unto holiness"*

139

(1 Thessalonians 4:7). The great plea against sin is that we are called to be holy. And the great power of holiness is that it is God's will for us.

And what is holiness? God alone is the Holy One. No one is holy except the Lord. There is no holiness but His. And nothing can be holy except as He makes it holy. *"Be ye holy; for I am holy"* (1 Peter 1:16). *"I am the* LORD *that doth sanctify you"* (Exodus 31:13). Holiness is the very nature of God, inseparable from His being. It can only be communicated by His communicating Himself and His own life. We are in Christ, who is made of God unto us sanctification. The Spirit of God is the Spirit of Holiness. We are God's *"elect...through sanctification of the Spirit"* (1 Peter 1:2), *"chosen...to salvation through sanctification of the Spirit"* (2 Thessalonians 2:13).

The Trinity is the Thrice Holy One: The Father, Son, and Spirit each share in making us holy. Our part in sanctification consists of our recognizing how God makes us holy. We have been sanctified in Christ Jesus. The new nature we have derived from Him has been created in true holiness. Our holy calling is the power of the new, divine, holy nature, to act out its impulses and principles. Our justification and our sanctification are equally in Christ—by union with Him—and therefore equally of faith. It is as we believe in God working in us, through Christ and the Spirit, that the inflow of the holy life from above is renewed. Thus, we have the courage and the power to live out the precepts that reveal the way in which the holy life is to be lived.

Like the whole of salvation, sanctification (or the life of holiness) is the result of man's cooperating with God. First of all, that means his entire dependence on and surrender to the divine operation as the only source of goodness or strength. And, then, it means the acting out in life and conduct all that God has worked within us.

And what encouragement can we find in the words—*"This is the will of God...your sanctification"*? The first thought is that of *the divine obligation of holiness.* God wills it. It is enough to compel us to consider the other aspects in which it can be presented. It is indeed an essential element of the Christian life and the great proof of our gratitude for deliverance from the guilt of sin. It is indispensable to true peace and happiness, our only preparation for heaven.

All this is of great importance. But behind all of this, there is something of still greater force. We need to realize that God wills it. In eternity, God predestinated us to be holy, we are *"elect according to the foreknowledge of God the Father, through sanctification of the*

Spirit" (1 Peter 1:2). God's whole purpose as a holy God was to make us holy as He is holy. The whole of redemption was ordered with this in mind. It is not only one of His commands; it is the command that includes all. The whole being and character of God proclaim it; the whole nature and aim of redemption insist upon it.

Believers, God wills your sanctification! Worship God in His holiness until every thought of God in His glory and grace is connected with the deep conviction: This blessed God wills my holiness. Do not rest until your will has surrendered unconditionally to the will of God and found its true destiny in receiving that divine will and working it out.

A second thought that suggests itself is that of *the divine possibility of holiness.* We have learned in our meditations that the will of God is more than a divine purpose of what God is to do or a divine precept as to what we are to do. It is also a divine power that works out its own purpose. All that God wills He works. But He does not do so in those who refuse to accept or submit to that will. They have the power to resist it. But in those who yield their consent, who love that will and long for it to be done on earth as in heaven, God works out all things after the purpose of His will. In every man with a sound, strong will, God's will seeks to embody itself in action and to bring about that which has been counted an object of desire.

God works in us both to will and to do. When He has worked the willing, He delights—if He is waited on and yielded to—to work the doing. When, by His grace, the believer wills as God wills—when he has accepted God's will for sanctification as his own will—he can count upon God's working it. God wills it with all the energy of His divine being. He can as little cease working holiness as He can cease being holy or being God. He wills our sanctification. And if we will it and yield ourselves to it, in the faith of the new nature that the Holy Spirit works, we can be assured that we will experience how true and blessed the message is. God wills, and therefore most certainly works, your sanctification.

The third lesson suggested by our text is *the divine meaning of holiness.* The will of God is your sanctification—that is, all that God wills has this one object and will secure this one result. Whether it is His will in the eternal counsel, in mercy, in judgment, in precept, or in promise, all that God wills concerning us is our sanctification. This gives a new meaning, and its true glory, to every command of Scripture. The commands of God have unspeakable value. They mark the path of safety and of life and guide us to all that is lovely and of good report. But here is their highest glory: Through them the Holy One seeks to make us partakers of His own holiness. Do let us learn to regard every indication of God's will, in Scripture or in nature, in things great or small, as the will of the Holy One coming to make us holy. Let every thought of God's will fill us with the longing and the hope of being holy. And let every thought of holiness lead us to the study of, the delight in, and the faithful doing of God's will. Let every sin that God's Word forbids, such as those Paul mentioned of uncleanness and fraud, be put far from us. Let everything that is of the earthly, carnal, selfish nature be put off, so that the whole spirit, soul, and body may be sanctified. Let every command that points to the true Christ-like life—humility, love, and self-sacrifice—be welcomed as the channel of God's holiness. The desire after, and the delight and faith in God's holiness and God's will, become inseparably one.

Let all who want to experience this remember one thing. It is because it is *God's* will and *God's* holiness that there is power, life, and blessing in it. Everything depends on our knowing God, waiting on Him, and coming under the operation of His holy presence and power. As we know Him as the Living God, have fellowship with Him as the holy, loving, almighty, ever-present, and ever-working One,

His will and His holiness will become heavenly realities to the believer. Then, we will know how certainly, how blessedly, His will is our sanctification.

Chapter 22
Unceasing Thanksgiving

"In everything give thanks: for this is the will of God in Christ Jesus concerning you."
—1 Thessalonians 5:18

"I*n everything give thanks*"—that means a life of unceasing joy. The giving of a gift makes me glad. Giving thanks is the expression of that gladness to the giver. For what he has given to me, and for how he has proven himself to be my friend, my happiness offers him all that it has to give.

Every father does his utmost to make his children happy. He not only loves to see them happy, but loves to see them associate their happiness with himself and his love. It is the will of God that in everything—in every circumstance and situation—the life of His child be one of unceasing praise and thanksgiving. If it is not always so with us, let us make every effort to learn the lesson: *"In everything give thanks: for this is the will of God in Christ Jesus concerning you."*

"In everything give thanks." There is good reason for it. God is not a hard master who reaps where He has not sown. He never commands joy without giving abundant cause for it. He does not expect thanks where there is nothing to be thankful for. He wants us to remember that, even in the most trying circumstances and the deepest sorrow, there is always more reason to be thankful than to be in mourning. Whatever we lose, God and His love are still with us. The very loss is meant to make the love more precious. The trial is actually love seeking to give itself more completely to us.

Whatever we lose, we always have the unspeakable gift—God's own Son—to be our portion and our friend. Whatever we lose, we will always have a peace that cannot be taken away, a joy that is unspeakable, a richness of glory that will supply every need, and an abounding grace that perfects Christ's strength in our weakness. There are always the exceedingly great and precious promises and the heavenly treasures that can never pass away. God is educating us, through loss and trial, into the full enjoyment of our heavenly heritage. He is perfectly preparing us for His own fellowship. So let us believe that the command is most reasonable and say that this will of God—*"in everything give thanks"*—is our will too.

"In everything give thanks." This is both the mark and the means of a vigorous Christian life. It draws us out of ourselves and fixes our hearts upon God. It lifts us above the world and makes us more than conquerors through Him who loves us (Romans 8:37). It places our peace, our happiness, our life, beyond the reach of circumstances. So far from rendering us indifferent to the suffering of our fellowmen, it fills us with hope in seeking to relieve them. It teaches us what joy there is in the kindness and love of God and makes that the keynote of our life. It gives wings to our prayer, our faith, and our love. It helps us to live the true heavenly life in God's presence and worship. It enables us to conquer every temptation with the hallelujah of victory.

"In everything give thanks." God Himself will work it in you. *"This is the will of God in Christ Jesus concerning you."* We have seen more than once that the will of God is a living, almighty power, working out its own purpose with our consent. We are coworkers with God; that means, not that He does part and we do part, but that He does all in us, and we do all through Him. It means that He works in us to will and to do, and that we—through faith in

His working, in the power that works in us—work out His will. Just because it is the will of God, the believing soul is sure that it can be.

"This is the will of God in Christ." This expression is so frequent that its meaning is often overlooked. All that God is and does to us, He is and does through our Lord Jesus. The Father does nothing in us but through the Son. The Son does nothing except as the Father does it through Him. Our experience of God's work in us depends on our abiding in Christ—our drawing and remaining near to God in and through Christ. To a soul seeking its life in Christ alone, the will of God ensures a life of unceasing praise and thanks.

"In everything give thanks." God's will needs a life of entire consecration. Many of God's commands become an unbearable burden or an impossible strain because we think our weak, sickly lives must do what only the strength of vigorous health can perform. We cannot take up one part of God's will and do it when we please. A life of undivided and absolute surrender to all God's will is necessary to be able to perform any part of it effectively. Every command to perform some special part of God's will is a call to inquire whether or not we have accepted all His will as the law of our life.

The soul that has done this—a soul that is learning the lesson of daily guidance for daily duty and is prepared to meet every new demand by questioning its implicit submission to that will—has found the secret of obedience to this command as well. He will know unquestioning confidence in the provision of sufficient strength to perform that will. When God is known as our exceeding joy, when a walk in the light of His countenance all the day is counted equally a privilege and an indispensable necessity, the giving of thanks in everything is not looked on as a hopeless attainment. Because it is the will of a loving and almighty Father, that will can be done.

"In everything give thanks." These are indeed the Christians the world stands in need of. It is the happy Christian—not the happy man who happens also to be a Christian, but the Christian who proves that his happiness is in God—who will find the joy of the Lord his strength in God's service. The Christian who lives the life of joy and praise because he lives in God's presence will be the best witness to what the grace of God can do to give true joy and blessing. It is the will of God in Christ to us that this unceasing thanksgiving should be our life—let us rest content with nothing less.

Chapter 23
The Salvation of All

"I exhort therefore, that, first of all, supplications, prayers, intercessions, and giving of thanks be made for all men....This is good and acceptable in the sight of God our Saviour, who will have all men to be saved."
—1 Timothy 2:1, 3–4

"The Lord is not slack concerning his promise, as some men count slackness; but is longsuffering to us-ward, not willing that any should perish, but that all should come to repentance."
—2 Peter 3:9

After Paul urged that supplications, prayers, and intercessions would *"be made for all men,"* he reminded us that we may do so in confident assurance that it is good and acceptable to God. He wills that *all* men would be saved. The knowledge and faith of God's will for all is to be the motivation and the measure of our prayer for all. What God in heaven wills and works for His children on earth, we are to will and work for too. As we enter into His will for all, we will know what we are to do to fulfill that will. And as we pray and labor for all, the faith in His will for all will inspire us with confidence and love.

Perhaps the question arises—If God wills the salvation of all, why is it not happening? What about the doctrine of election, as Scripture teaches us? And what about the omnipotence of God, which is surely equal to His love that wills the salvation of all? As to election, remember that there are mysteries in God and in Scripture that are beyond our reach. If there are apparently conflicting truths that we cannot reconcile, we know that Scripture was not written, like a book of science, to satisfy the intellect. It is the revelation of the hidden wisdom of God, which tests and strengthens faith and submission and awakens love and childlike teachableness.

If we cannot understand why His power does not work what His will has purposed, we will find that all that God does or does not do is decided by conditions far beyond our human comprehension. It requires a divine wisdom to grasp and to order God's ways. We will learn that God's will is as much beyond our comprehension as God's being. And it is our wisdom, safety, and happiness to accept every revealed truth with the simplicity and the faith of little children. We must yield ourselves to it to prove its living power within our hearts. Let us not fear to yield ourselves to the utmost to this blessed word: *"God...will have all men to be saved."*

God is love. His will is love. As He makes His sun to shine on the good and the evil, so His love rests on all. However little we can understand why His love is so long-suffering and patient, we can believe in and be assured of the love that God gives to us—love whose measure in heaven is the gift of His Son and on earth every child of man. His love is nothing but His will in its divine energy doing its very utmost in accordance with the divine law. Thus, His relationship to mankind is regulated to make men partakers of His blessedness. His will is nothing but His love in its infinite patience and tenderness delighting to win and bless every heart into which it can gain access.

If we only knew God and His love, how we would look on every man we see as one upon whom that love rests and for whom it longs. We would begin to wonder about the mystery of grace that has taken up the church—making it the body of Christ and a partner in the great work of showing God's love—a grace that is dependent upon the church's faithfulness. And we would see that all who live to do God's will must believe this to be its central glory: Our doing the will that wills that all men would be saved.

"God...will have all men to be saved." This truth is a supernatural mystery. It can only be understood by a spiritual mind through the teaching of the Holy Spirit. It is in itself so divine and beyond our apprehension—the difficulties that surround it are so many and so real—that it needs so much time and sacrifice to master its teaching. To very many who do not possess a humble, loving heart, the words carry little meaning.

To the believer, who in very deed seeks to know and to do all God's will, God's words give a new meaning to life. He begins to see that this call to love and to save his fellow-men is not something accidental or additional. He begins to realize that, along with the other things that make up his life, he can devote as much time and thought to this as he sees fit. He learns that just as this loving, saving will of God is the secret source of all his will and rules it all, so this loving, saving will is to be the chief thing that he lives for too. I have been redeemed, organically united to, and made a member of the saving Christ, who came to do this will of the Father.

I have been chosen and set apart and fitted for this as the one object of my being in the world. I begin to see that the prayer, *"Thy will be done"* (Matthew 6:10) means, above everything else, that I give myself for this loving, saving will of God to possess, inspire, use, and if need be, consume me. And I feel the need of spelling out the words of the sentence until my heart can call them its own: *"God"*—my God, who lives in me—*"will have"*—with His whole heart, in that will that He has revealed to His people that they may carry it into effect—*"all men"*—here around me, and to the ends of the earth—*"to be saved"*—to have everlasting life.

Paul wrote these words in connection with a call to prayer for all men. Our faith in the truth of God's loving, saving will must be put into practice. It must stir us to prayer. And prayer will most certainly stir us to work. We must not only seek to believe and feel the truth of these words, but we must also act. This will of God must be done. Let us look upon those around us as the objects of God's love, whom His saving will is seeking to reach. Let us, as we yield ourselves to this will, go and speak to those around us about God's love in Christ.

It is possible that we are not succeeding in doing God's will in our personal lives because we neglect the chief thing. As we pray to be possessed and filled with the knowledge of God's will, let us seek, in all things, to have our hearts filled with this love. Let us have tongues that speak of Jesus and His salvation, and a will that finds its strength in God's own will—that all men be saved. So will our life, our love, our work, and our will in some measure be like that of Jesus Christ—a doing of the Father's will, that none of these little ones should perish.

Chapter 24
Lo, I Come to Do Thy Will

"Then said I, Lo, I come to do thy will, O God....By the which will we are sanctified through the offering of the body of Jesus Christ once for all."
—Hebrews 10:7, 10

"Lo, I come...I delight to do thy will, O my God."
—Psalm 40:7–8

David had said, *"Sacrifice and offering thou didst not desire"* (Psalm 40:6). They were not what God sought or what could please Him. They were not really the will of God. David understood that what God wanted was the doing of His will and said, *"I delight to do thy will, O my God."* While saying this of himself, he spoke it of Christ, in whom alone its true fulfillment could be found. They are the

159

great words with which Christ coming into the world announces His work: *"Lo, I come to do thy will, O God."* If we are really to penetrate to the very heart of what Christ is and means, of what He did for us and does in us, we must seek to know Him as come from heaven to earth to do the will of God. In this way, He is to restore the doing of God's will on earth to the place it has in heaven.

His doing of God's will is first contrasted with the sacrifices and offerings of Old Testament worship, and then it is specially connected with the offering of His own body once and for all. Of this will of God, as thus done by Him even unto death, we are taught that in it we have been sanctified. By one offering, He has forever perfected those who are sanctified. Let us try to learn the great lessons that are to be found here in connection with our study of the will of God.

The doing of God's will is the only worship that is pleasing to God. It was this alone that gave value to the Old Testament sacrifices. Not in the costliness or the multitude of the offerings did they find their value, but in the disposition, contrition, faith, or consecration in which they were the expressed. Their value was not even in these, however, except as they were a divine appointment and were brought in accordance with God's own command.

If not accompanied by obedience, they were worse than useless. *"To obey is better than sacrifice"* (1 Samuel 15:22). *"Thou delightest not in burnt offering. The sacrifices of God are a broken spirit: a broken and a contrite heart"* (Psalm 51:16–17). It is as far as they were doing God's will that they were well-pleasing. And so they became the symbols of a life given up in devotion to God, wholly yielded to His will and service. The doing of God's will is the secret of acceptable worship.

Christ came to this world to do the will of God. He came and lived as a man to show us that the one thing God asks, and the one thing that can bring life and blessedness, is doing the will of God. With this view, He submitted Himself to more than all the commandments and ordinances of the law. In all His life and work, in His eating and speaking, in His travels and miracles, He lived a life of absolute dependence on God's guidance. In everything, He did only God's will; He did all God's will.

Our Lord knew that it was God's will that He would die as a propitiation for our sins. As the time came near, and all the implications opened up before His human nature, He had more than one occasion to say: "How I am distressed! How My soul is troubled! My soul is sorrowful even unto death!" (See Matthew 26:38.) But through it all, He thought of God's will. The surrender to God's will sustained Him. And He gave Himself to be what the sin offering and burnt offering had only typified—a sacrifice unto God, obedient even unto death. It was this that gave His inconceivable suffering its inconceivable value. It was borne as the will of God, laying God's just judgment on Him so that the guilty might go free.

It is Christ's doing the will of God even unto death that has affected our salvation. "By the which will we are sanctified through the offering of the body of Jesus Christ once for all." The word *"sanctified"* is used here in its larger sense, as it includes justification, regeneration, and the whole of redemption. It refers to our being restored to the fellowship of God and taken possession of by Him. The great sin of Adam and of mankind was doing their own will instead of God's will. The great and only root of all sin and misery was self-will. Jesus Christ came to take away sin. He did so by a life and a death of the most perfect sacrifice of His will to the will of God. He bore the consequence, the punishment, and the curse that our self-will had brought.

Through Christ's perfect obedience to the Father's will, He made a perfect atonement for our sin and won a place of supremacy in the sinful world for the will of God. He did this by the offering of His body, once and for all, and so forever perfected those who are sanctified.

"By the obedience of one shall many be made righteous" (Romans 5:19). As partakers of a complete and perfect righteousness, won by obedience to the will of God, as *"ye put on the new man, which after God is created in righteousness"* (Ephesians 4:24), our entrance into the perfect love and life of God is complete and forever.

The doing of God's will by which Christ brought about our salvation is now and forever the power of the salvation He imparts. Doing God's will is not only, as many think, the price by which salvation was won. Doing God's will is salvation itself. In Christ, it was the power that conquered every temptation to self-will. It proved what human life really ought to be like. It brought about a perfect human life and laid it as a sacrifice at God's feet. It was God's will in Christ that forever broke the power of self-will and its dominion over us. In Christ, it proved that sacrificing self-will to the very utmost—doing the will of God even unto death—is the path to the fullness of the life and glory of God. In Christ, doing the will of God is seen to be the life and joy of heaven brought down to earth and the power to rise from earth to heaven. Doing God's will is at once the cause, the object, the power, and the blessedness of salvation.

It is only by Christ in us that we can in any way do the will of God on earth as it is done in heaven. The prayer that Christ taught us was meant to be heard; God answers it in various degrees. To pray it daily means to aim at it in the faith of God's answer. And yet how many earnest Christians are utterly hopeless in regard to it. Their surrender to do God's will is continually failing. They fail because they are attempting to do it in the power of a life that is not wholly possessed by Jesus Christ. Listen to His Word: *"Lo, I come to do Thy will."* All power to do God's will is in Him. As we can truly say, Christ lives in me, we will find His strength perfected in our weakness.

Each believer is called, as one sanctified in the will of God by the offering of the body of Jesus Christ, to accept the will of God as done by Christ for us. And it is still being done in us by Him as God's free gift in Christ Jesus. The one thing needed, once the heart sees, accepts, loves, and vows this doing of God's will as its one desire, is the faith that Jesus does take charge of a surrendered will. Believe, in the power of Him who lives in heaven and lives in us, that the doing of God's will can become our daily life.

Chapter 25
Obtaining the Promise

"Ye have need of patience, that, after ye have done the will of God, ye might receive the promise."
—Hebrews 10:36

It was in a time of very severe trial that this epistle was addressed to the Hebrews. It had been a bitter disappointment for them to see their nation rejecting the Messiah. And for that, they were rejected by God. To have the temple, with its divine ordinances of circumcision and sacrifice, set aside was a mystery to many and a cause of deep sorrow. In reproach and the spoiling of their goods, they personally had to endure the pain of persecution.

The epistle was written to comfort them by revealing the spiritual glory of Christ's priesthood and the salvation He bestowed. And it pointed them to the Father, to prove that suffering had been the path of all God's saints and had always brought great reward. It is in this connection that the words come, *"Ye have need of patience, that, after ye have done the will of God, ye might receive the promise."* The promise was sure and very precious. The suffering was needful and would be very blessed. The one thing they needed was patience in bearing what God sent and in waiting for what He had promised. And in that time of patient waiting, they needed just one thing—to see that they did the will of God.

In a world of sorrow and trial, the Christian has just this one thing to strive for: not only to bear, but also to do the will of God. After you have done the will of God, you may receive the promise.

Doing the will of God is the path to the inheritance. The inheritance owes its divine glory and blessedness to God having willed it. God's will working in us can alone prepare us for receiving and enjoying it. And God's will can work in no other way than by our doing it, since we are endowed with intelligence, will, and moral powers. In the very nature and necessity of things, the only way of our receiving the promise, which has been bestowed of grace, is by our doing the will. We cannot earn or merit His promises. We have been looking at the will of God in various aspects. Let us once again turn to this, one of the most elementary, and yet one of the deepest, truths connected with it.

"Hav[ing] *done the will of God."* It has been said that the highest form of existence is the power to do work. It is so in God. All His attributes could not make Him the glorious God He is if they were all dormant, inactive powers. His love, for instance, would be a mere thought or sentiment, not a reality or a truth. The highest form of human existence is also the power to do work. And, as a human, the highest form of that power can be nothing other than working out the perfect will of God.

God works to will and to do in us. And what He works in us we work out, doing what He wills and does in us. Such doing of the will of God proves our entire surrender to it, our being truly mastered and possessed by it. Such doing of the will of God is what gives strength to our inner man, refines and spiritualizes our whole being, prepares us for being the dwelling place of the three-in-one God (John 14:15, 21, 23), and for entering into His abode hereafter (Matthew 7:21). Such doing of the will of God prepares a Christian for receiving every promise.

It was in the time of suffering and trial that these believers were thus to do the will of God. The first concern of most Christians in trouble is to be delivered from it. This may not be the most important thing to be concerned with. The one great desire ought to be never to fail in knowing or doing the will of God. This is the secret of strength and true nobility in the Christian life.

Some think that, if under reproach or persecution or injustice, evil feelings are roused and given way to. They believe that there is some excuse for it—it cannot be judged too severely—the temptation was so great. God's Word teaches us differently. It regards the Christian so entirely as a man who has given up his own will to live wholly for God's will that it says to him—of all trial and temptation of whatever nature—seek one thing: not to sin against God. Be patient, and see that you do the will of God.

But is this beyond human power—in every trial to always think first of God's will and do it? It is indeed something beyond human power, but not beyond the power of grace. It was for this reason that our Lord Jesus came to earth, saying: *"I come to do thy will, O God!"* (Hebrews 10:9) and went to the Cross with the cry, *"Not my will, but thine be done"* (Luke 22:42). He lived as an example of how we ought to live. He died to set us free from the power of sin and to open the path—through death to sin and self—to a life for God and His will. He ascended to heaven to give His own

Holy Spirit, so that in His power we might, like Him, do the will of the Father.

It is a shame that, in the church of Christ, so few know that to do the will of God is the first duty of the believer. And as a result of this, there is so little desire of the promise and the need of the Holy Spirit to teach us God's will in daily life. And still further, there is so little faith in the power of the grace of Christ and His Spirit to prepare us for the life of doing the will of God.

Men have lost sight of the supernatural light that reveals the will of God in its beauty and attractiveness and makes it a joy to do it. They do not feel the supernatural obligation to live wholly and entirely for the will of that God who created us, and to whom Christ has brought us back. They are unaware of the supernatural power—corresponding to the light and the obligation—that brings a life in the will of God within our reach, because Christ's strength is made perfect in our weakness.

Believer, whatever others say or do, take the Word in its simple, divine meaning, *"Ye have need of patience, that, after ye have done the will of God, ye might receive the promise."* Ask God, by His Holy Spirit—in the renewing of the spirit of your mind—to show you how He would have you live wholly in His will.

Yield yourself to that will in everything you know, and do it. Yield yourself to that will in all its divine love and quickening power as it works in you and makes you partaker of its innermost nature. Pray, pray, pray, until you increasingly see how what Christ revealed in His life and death is the promise and pledge of what God will work in you. Learn how your abiding in Him and your oneness with Him means nothing less than your being called to do the will of God as He did it.

Chapter 26
God Working His Will

"Now the God of peace...make you perfect in every good work to do his will, working in you that which is wellpleasing in his sight, through Jesus Christ; to whom be glory for ever and ever."
—Hebrews 13:20–21

In Hebrews, we have three passages on the will of God. The first, Hebrews 10:7–10, speaks of that will, and Christ's doing of it, as the cause of our redemption—the deep root in which our life stands. The second, Hebrews 10:36, speaks of that will as done patiently by us, amid the trials of this earth. The third, our present text, shows us the wondrous bond of union between the two former. The same God who worked out His will in Christ for our redemption is working out that will in us too. What God did in Christ is the pledge of what

He will do in us too. Christ's doing the will of God secures our doing that will too. Listen to the wondrous teaching.

> *Now, the God of peace, who brought again from the dead the Great Shepherd of the sheep in the blood of the everlasting covenant, even our Lord Jesus, make you perfect to do His will.*
> (Hebrews 13:20–21)

All that is said here about the Lord Jesus refers to the previous teaching of the epistle. We have been taught about the covenant, the blood of the covenant, and the exaltation to the throne of Christ as the Priest-King and the Great Shepherd of the sheep. And now, the epistle says that the God of peace, who did it all—who gave Christ to do His will and die on the cross and then raised Him from the dead—will also perfect us to do His will.

As much as it was God who sent and enabled Christ to do His will, and through that perfected Him and perfected our salvation, it is God who will also perfect us in every good thing to do His will. God's will being done in us interests God as much as His will done in Christ. He cares for the one as much as the other. The same omnipotence that created a body through the Virgin Mary, for Christ, and empowered Christ—who could do nothing of Himself—to do that will, is working in you that you may do His will. The same omnipotent God who was with Christ as He endured the agony of Gethsemane and the surrender of His Spirit into His Father's hand on Calvary and who then raised Him from the grave to His own right hand is also with you. Oh, for grace to believe this—the God who worked all in Christ, even raising Him from the dead, is working all in us!

You do not fully understand it yet. It looks altogether too impossible. The difference is too great. The difficulties in our sinful nature are too insurmountable. Come and listen once again. "Now, the God of peace, that brought again from the dead our Lord Jesus"—do pause, and take in every word—"make you perfect in every good work to do His will"! What more could one wish?

And yet, to remove all doubt, there is more. There follows, *"working in you that which is wellpleasing in his sight, through Jesus Christ."* The central words, to do His will, are held tightly between what precedes them— God Himself make you perfect in every good thing, and what follows: *"working in you that which is wellpleasing in His sight."* The connection between our doing and God's working is so wonderful. He prepares us in every good thing to do His will, so that the doing of it is really our work, and yet at the same time it is His own working in us. God fits us for the work and then works it through us. And so all is of God!

There are three lessons that we want to take into our heart and that we want to ask God to teach us by the Holy Spirit. The first is: *The one object of the great redemption is to make us ready to do God's will here on earth.* For that we were created; that was God's image and likeness in us. That was our fitness for fellowship with God and the participation in His rule of the world to which we were destined. To redeem and bring us back to this, God worked that stupendous miracle of power and of love. His Son became man so that He might show us how to do God's will and how, by doing it, sin could be atoned for and conquered. Christ lives in heaven and in our hearts so that God may work in us that which is well-pleasing in His heart. What the sinner needs to know when he is called to repentance, what the believer needs to be continually reminded of and encouraged in, is this: I have been redeemed to do God's will.

The failure in so many Christian lives is simply due to this—the church has not clearly and persistently preached the great message that all God's wondrous grace has this one object: to restore us to the original glory of our creation and make it our life to do His will.

174

The second lesson is no less important: *we can do God's will because God Himself prepares us for it, "working in [us] that which is wellpleasing in His sight."*

Alas, how little this is known or believed by believers! The call to do all God's will is negated by the terrible unbelief that says, "It cannot be; I cannot do it." Men say that they believe that all the mysteries of redemption, including Christ's resurrection and exhaltation to heaven, were brought about *"according to the working of his mighty power"*(Ephesians 1:19). But they do not believe what Scripture affirms just as distinctly, that the same exceeding greatness of His power works in those who believe.

Let me implore every child of God who wants to live to do His will to remember: The will of God is holy and divine. No one can do it but God Himself. God has given you a renewed will, capable of knowing, desiring, and even delighting in His will. But you are not capable of doing it in your own strength. The work of our will is to accept His will as being what He will indeed work in us. This is indeed our highest glory—that God, according to His very nature, must work all in all and will work in us both to will and to do. He Himself prepares us in every good thing to do His will, working in us that which is pleasing in His sight.

The last lesson follows naturally: *Our great need and duty, once we have accepted our calling to live only to do His will, is to bow before God in continual humility and dependence.* We must ask to fully know our utter inability and seek to trust confidently His power to work in us. And with this, we must understand that His power cannot work freely and fully in us, except as He dwells in us. Jesus said, "The Father abiding in Me does the works." (See John 14:10.) It is *"through Jesus Christ"* that God works in us what is pleasing in His sight. That is, through Jesus Christ dwelling in the heart, by the power of the Holy Spirit, the almighty God works out His will in us by fitting us to do it. The one necessary thing is, a simple, unceasing, and unlimited faith in the indwelling Jesus. *"Lo, I come"* (Hebrews 10:7), He said. *"I delight to do Thy will"* (Psalm 40:8). That is not only for us, but *in us*. He is the Executor of the Father's will, through whom that will is carried out.

Let us turn with a new consecration to do all God's will, and with a new faith in God who will work in us the ability to do it. With a new devotion to Jesus Christ, we the sinful, the weak, can indeed have grace to say, "I delight to do Your will, O my God."

Chapter 27
Suffering According to the Will of God

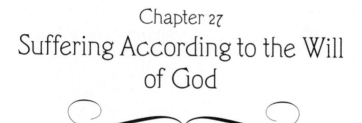

"For so is the will of God, that with well doing ye may put to silence the ignorance of foolish men.....If, when ye be buffeted for your faults, ye shall take it patiently... this is acceptable with God...because Christ also suffered for us, leaving us an example, that ye should follow his steps."
—1 Peter 2:15, 20–21

"It is better, if the will of God be so, that ye suffer for well doing, than for evil-doing. For Christ also hath once suffered for sins."
—1 Peter 3:17–18

"But rejoice, inasmuch as ye are partakers of Christ's sufferings....Wherefore let them that suffer according to the will of God commit the

keeping of their souls to him in well doing, as unto a faithful Creator."
—1 Peter 4:13–19

Before Peter had received the Holy Spirit, he did not understand that suffering had to be borne as God's will. When Christ spoke of His suffering, Peter reproved Him and had to bear the rebuke, *"Get thee behind me, Satan"* (Matthew 16:23). When his discipleship brought him into danger and suffering, he denied his Lord. He could not see that suffering was God's will. With Pentecost, everything was changed. He knew no fear. He rejoiced that he was counted worthy to suffer for Christ's name. In his epistle, he continually connected Christ's suffering for our sins with His example, calling us to suffer like Him. "Through suffering to glory" is the keynote of his exhortation to the saints. Let us listen to what he teaches us about the will of God in suffering.

The first lesson is: *To regard all suffering as the will of God for us. "If the will of God be so, that ye suffer for well doing." "Them that suffer according to the will of God."* He spoke about suffering injustice at the hands of our fellowmen. Very many who think they are ready to endure trial that comes directly from God find it difficult to bear unkind, hard, or unjust treatment from men. And yet, it is here that Christ's teaching, example, and all

178

Scripture instruction call us to accept and bow to the will of God.

Whether it is in the most flagrant injustice, the most terrible suffering—such as our Lord endured at the hands of Caiaphas and Pilate—or the smaller vexations that we meet with in daily life from enemies or friends, all suffering must be to us the will of God. Nothing can come to us without the will of God. What is done may be contrary to the will of God, and the doer may be guilty in His sight, but that it is done to us—that we suffer by it—is God's will. And the first duty of the child of God is not to look at the man who does it or to seek to be avenged of him or to be delivered from his hands, but to recognize and bow beneath it as the Father's will. That one thought—it is the Father's will—changes our feelings toward it. It enables us to accept it as a blessing and changes it from an evil to a good. In all suffering, let our first thought be to see the Father's hand and to count on the Father's help. Then no circumstance whatever can, for one moment, take us out of the blessed will of God.

The second lesson is: *Ever to suffer with well doing.* In all three texts, the words *well doing* occur. If we suffer when we do wrong, and bear it patiently, this is no glory. The one thing we are to care for is that, if we suffer, it is not to be for wrongdoing, but for well doing.

179

For it is better, if the will of God be so, that you suffer for well doing than for evil doing. And along with well doing, we must allow the suffering to call forth anything sinful. That must be our one desire in suffering. It is caused by sin, and it is meant to take away sin. How terrible if I make it the occasion of more sin and turn it into the very opposite of what God means it to be.

But if we suffer when we do well and take it patiently, this is acceptable with God— that by well doing we put to silence the ignorance of foolish men. Men may learn from us what the power of grace is—to soften and to strengthen. They will learn the reality of the heavenly life and joy that enables us to bear all loss. They will discover what the blessing of the service of the divine Master, who can make His own path of suffering so attractive and so blessed to His followers, is. And it is in well doing that we can commit our souls to a faithful Creator.

Here is the third lesson: *In suffering, to commit our souls to God's faithful keeping.* What a precious privilege! Amid all the temptation suffering brings, God Himself offers to take charge of the keeping of our souls. Going down into the darkness of death, our Lord Jesus said, *"Father, into thy hands I commend my spirit"* (Luke 23:46). Into every dark cloud of suffering that we enter, we may say this too.

From all the strife of tongues and the pride of man, from our tendency to be impatient or angry, to judge quickly, or to be unloving, the faithful Creator can keep the soul committed to Him. He who sends the suffering as His will has beforehand provided a place of safety. That is where the blessing of the suffering will assuredly be given. Let us say, *"I know whom I have believed, and am persuaded that he is able to keep that which I have committed unto him"* (2 Timothy 1:12).

Then comes the last lesson: *In all our suffering according to the will of God, Christ is our example and our strength.* In all three chapters, Christ suffering for our sake is connected with our suffering for His sake. *"Christ also suffered for us, leaving us an example, that ye should follow his steps." "It is better...that ye suffer for well doing...for Christ also hath once suffered for sins."*

> *Forasmuch then as Christ hath suffered for us in the flesh, arm yourselves likewise with the same mind....But rejoice, inasmuch as ye are partakers of Christ's sufferings...for the spirit of glory and of God resteth upon you.* (1 Peter 4:1, 13–14)

The sufferings of believers are as indispensable as those of Christ are. They are to be borne in the same spirit. They are the means of fellowship with Him and conformity to His image. Christ Jesus accepted and bore all suffering of whatever nature—great or small, whether coming in the ordinary course of events or especially devised against Him—as the will of God. He endured all as the necessary result of sin, in submission to the will of the Father who sent it, as the school in which He was to prove that His will was one with the Father's and that the Father's will was over all.

Christ is our pattern, because He is our life. In time of suffering, the Spirit of glory and the Spirit of God rest on us. Oh, that all believers who desire to live wholly in the will of God might understand how much depends on their recognizing God's will in all suffering. They must bear all according to the will of God. And may they understand too, how impossible it is to disconnect Christ's sufferings for us from ours for Him. He suffered for us as our Head, in whom we are made alive. We can only suffer for Him as He lives in us.

Attempting to do or bear the will of God correctly, as long as we are living on a different level from that on which Christ lived, will result in failure. It is only where the wholehearted surrender to live and die for the will of God, as He did, possesses the soul that the mighty power of His love, grace, and Spirit can do their wonders in the life of the believer.

Chapter 28
Living to the Will of God

"That he no longer should live the rest of his time in the flesh to the lusts of men, but to the will of God."
—1 Peter 4:2

The believers to whom Peter wrote needed to be reminded that there is a twofold possibility in the Christian life. It is possible, even after conversion, to still live *"to the lusts of men,"* desiring and seeking what men in the world seek. It is possible, on the other hand, to turn entirely away from living to the desires of men, and wholly live to the will of God, even as Christ had done. He had written, *"Forasmuch then as Christ hath suffered for us in the flesh, arm yourselves likewise with the same mind: for he that hath suffered in the flesh hath ceased from sin"* (1 Peter 4:1). He then continued, as the fruit of the previous verse,

"No longer should live the rest of his time in the flesh to the lusts of men, but to the will of God" (1 Peter 4:2).

Every Christian stands between the two contending forces. The unceasing influence of human nature and its desires, the example of the men of the world, and the whole current of human society draws him to live to the desires of men. Blessed is the man who has yielded himself to the power of Christ and His cross, and who has armed himself with the same mind, to suffer at any cost rather than to sin. Blessed is he who now lives as Christ, not to the will of man, but to the will of God. Blessed is the life in which the purpose of Christ's coming is being realized and that is now wholly yielded to, inspired, and controlled by the will of God.

We are approaching the close of our study of the will of God as our dwelling place. We have had occasion to look at it from almost every possible side. The desire, the hope, and the purpose to live only to the will of God may be awakened or strengthened in many a heart. And yet, there may be a painful sense of failure and a consciousness that there is some hidden trouble that hinders the possession of what appears to be so clearly promised in God's Word. Let me try to gather up all the teaching we have had and point out, in the simplest way possible, what steps lead to the life

Scripture teaches us to pray for and expect— perfect and complete in all the will of God.

1. I must first mention what often comes last in experience: *To live in God's will is impossible except as we live in close and abiding fellowship with Jesus Christ.* It is He who proclaimed, *"Lo, I am come to do thy will, O God"* (Hebrews 10:7). He not only had to do it alone on Calvary: The work He began there He carries on in heaven. Today, still, it is through Him alone that God works His will in us. (See Hebrews 13:21.) It is impossible to bear or do God's will as Christ did, except as we have the same mind that was in Him. And we cannot have the same mind, except as we are wholly given up to Him, have Him living in us, and seek to live in His fellowship.

   It is the living presence and power of Christ in the heart that enables us to do God's will from the heart. You cannot demand a sickly life to do the work of a healthy man. When the sufficiency of Christ's grace is known, and our strength is made perfect in weakness because His power rests upon us, we can truly live for God.

2. *To live to God's will demands that there be a clear and full surrender of every moment of our life to that will.* Failure arises when

we do not see how God's will fits into the little, natural, innocent things of life. We need to pray very earnestly for a spiritual insight into the blessed truth that every power, every moment, and every movement of our life must be in harmony with His will. We are so slow to comprehend what this means that, unless we offer patient, persevering prayer and a very docile waiting for the Spirit's teaching, we may struggle for years without grasping what ought to be an elementary truth: God's will must rule our life as it ruled the life of Christ Jesus. All must be according to the will of God.

3. *To live to God's will, it is essential that whatever we know to be according to that will be done at once.* Until we have the power to do all God's will, it is easy to be tempted to think that a small failure— additional to those that appear necessary—is not of much consequence. Some make the mistake of thinking that, as long as they have not received some special endowment of power, it is needless and vain to attempt a perfect obedience. Let us beware of giving way to such thoughts. All increase of grace and strength in the Christian life stands under the law of faithfulness in little things. Whatever you know to be the will of God, little or great,

do it at once. If you are not sure, do the nearest to what you know to be right. It is in doing what we know that we prove our integrity and are prepared to receive more grace.

4. *Learn also to do all your ordinary works as the will of God.* There is such a vast range of ordinary, everyday duty or drudgery that appears to have little direct connection with the will of God and is, therefore, unconsciously separated from it. Beware of giving way to this. Study Paul and Peter's wonderful teaching to the mistreated slaves of their day. (See chapters 19 and 27 of this book.) They called upon them to perform their entire service and bear all their sufferings from hard masters *as God's will!* And this was to be done from the heart, as unto the Lord! Once all the work of our daily calling is seen to be God's will and is done heartily for His sake, it no longer needs to be a hindrance. It will become a great help in enabling us to live wholly to the will of God.

5. *Let no secret misunderstanding of the doctrine of our entire inability, and the impossibility of a life truly well-pleasing to God, hinder you.* Jesus Christ said, "'My grace is sufficient for thee' (2 Corinthians 12:9), for all I ask of you, for all you have to do." Our nature is utterly corrupt and ineffective.

In our flesh dwells no good thing. Living to God's will is only possible by the power of Jesus Christ resting on us and working in us through the Holy Spirit. Get a firm hold on the truth that God's Spirit dwells in you as the power for you to do God's will. The grace of the Spirit is only known as you act it out, that is, as in faith you try to do what appears to be too great for your weakness. Only believe is also the law for living to the will of God.

6. *To live to God's will, you need to wait daily for the divine guidance of the Holy Spirit to make that will known to you.* Many pray for divine strength to do God's will but do not first think of a divine light to know God's will. God's will as taught by men or books does not have the power to influence. A supernatural teaching awakens the need, and gives the promise, of a supernatural power. The will of God is not a number of laws and rules. It is a living light and power, revealed in fellowship with Him. The believer who truly wants to live to the will of God in all things will deeply feel the need of a divine guidance leading him day by day in the path and the steps of our Lord Jesus. Oh, let us no longer live to the will of man but to the will of God!

Chapter 29
The Secret of Abiding

"If any man love the world, the love of the Father is not in him....And the world passeth away, and the lust thereof: but he that doeth the will of God abideth for ever."
—1 John 2:15, 17

Once again, we have here the contrast between the two great powers that contend for mastery over man. We saw, in Romans 12:2, how the great danger that threatens the consecrated man, and makes a life in God's will impossible, comes from the side of worldly conformity. And in Galatians 1:4, we saw how the one great aim of God's will in the death of Christ was to deliver us from this present, evil world. The irreconcilable hostility of the two principles is brought out here with equal force. *"If any man love the world, the love of the Father is not in him."*

Freedom from the love of the world, by the love of the Father utterly expelling it, is the law of the normal Christian life. And the exercise and discipline by which the true position is to be maintained, with the love of the Father and not the love of the world filling the heart and life, is the doing of the will of God. *"He that doeth the will of God abideth for ever"*—abides unchangeably in God and in unchangeable love.

What sacred associations are connected with that word abiding! Abiding in Christ and in His love (John 15); abiding in the Son and in the Father (1 John 2:24–28); God and Christ, the truth and the anointing abiding in us (1 John 2:14–27; 3:24). The main thought is permanent, steadfast, and immovable continuance in the place and the blessing secured to us in Christ and God. The great secret of the world is its transitoriness—it passes away with all its glory. And all who are of it partake of its vanity and uncertainty. And just as far as the Christian breathes its spirit and allows its love a place in his heart, he loses the power of abiding.

All failure in abiding—all lack of permanence and perseverance in the Christian life—can have no other cause than that the spirit and life of the world are robbing the soul of its real and only strength. The Word and will of God are unchangeable and eternal: He who does the will of God abides forever. As a man does the will of God, and in doing, appropriates it—feeds on and assimilates it—its very essence enters into his being. He becomes partaker of its divine strength and unchangeableness.

As the life of God is, so is His will—without variableness and shadow of turning. And as the will of God is taken up into the life of the believer, it is also changed into the likeness of the divine life and becomes freed from all the variableness that is the mark of this world. *"The world passeth away...he that doeth the will of God abideth for ever."*

"He that doeth the will of God." It is by *doing* that the will of God enters into us and communicates its own divine unchangeableness. The revelation by the Spirit, as well as the knowledge and contemplation of the love and adoration of the will of God—all these have their place and value. But it is not until we have really *done* and are continually *doing* the will of God that it has really mastered us— conquered every enemy—and transformed us into the perfect likeness of itself. It is as the doing of the Father's will becomes our meat— the satisfaction of our soul's hunger and our nourishment—that God Himself becomes the strength of our life. It is only then that man is brought back to his original glory.

God's Will: Our Dwelling Place

Man was created with a will, that into it he might receive the will of God. In that way, God might work His will into him; and so man, in working that will out again, might become the partner and fellow worker with God in all His works. Jesus Christ, as man, restored human nature to its ideal destiny and proved what blessedness and glory it is to live only to do the will of God. And redeemed men receive the Spirit of Jesus Christ so that they, even as He, might find their life in accepting, living, and doing nothing but the will of God.

As God's will is the only power that upholds and secures the existence of the universe, so that will, done by the believer, is the one security that he never will be moved. The whole of redemption—all that it reveals about pardoning, sanctifying, and preserving grace—has this as its aim and its crown: that man would find his blessedness in, his fellowship with, and his likeness to God in doing His will. *"He that doeth the will of God abideth for ever."*

Blessed abiding! How often believers have mourned and wondered about why there was so little abiding peace and joy in their life. They wondered why their abiding in Christ and His life was so fluctuating and uncertain. They did not know how near the answer lay: *"He that doeth the will of God abideth for ever."* They never noticed how distinctly our Lord had made this the one condition of abiding in Him: *"If ye keep my commandments, ye shall abide in my love; even as I have kept my Father's commandments, and abide in his love"* (John 15:10).

Could words make it any plainer that obedience—doing His will—is the secret of abiding? If, instead of occupying ourselves with abiding as being the object of direct desire, faith, prayer, and effort, we were to give ourselves up wholly to keep the commandments and do the will, the abiding would come by itself. It would be given to us by a secret power from on high. *"He that doeth the will of God abideth for ever"* and will always and unceasingly abide.

In the teaching of the church of Christ, and in the life of a great majority of believers, the doing of the will of the Father does not have the overwhelming prominence that it had in the life and teaching of Christ—as in the purpose of the Father. Any revival that is to really affect the spiritual life and elevate the standard of Christian living must be a revival of holy living. It must include the vindication of God's claim that every child of His should give himself God's will on earth as it is done in heaven.

Once God's claim is fully admitted and unconditionally accepted, divine guidance will lead us to His will. Then, we will experience the divine power that makes it possible, the divine certainty that it will be done. Everything depends on simple and wholehearted acceptance of the great truth: To be brought back to do the will of God is the one thing we have been redeemed for. Doing that will is, on earth as in heaven, with us as with our Lord Jesus, the one secret of abiding in the love of God.

Chapter 30
Praying According to God's Will

"And this is the confidence that we have in him, that, if we ask any thing according to his will, he heareth us: and if we know that he hear us, whatsoever we ask, we know that we have the petitions that we desired of him."
—1 John 5:14–15

God works out His will through the willing and doing of His people. He works in them, unconsciously to them, both to will and to do. While they study His will in His Word, and take it up into their wills and lives and work it out, He is working it out through them. It is a heart and life filled with the love of God's will that becomes the prepared instrument through which God can do His work.

It is with prayer as it is with work. As God has taken the cooperation and the labor of

His people into His eternal purpose, so their prayers too. Prayer's origin lies in our desires as awakened by our need or by God's promises; and yet, they are God's own working in us. They cannot effect any change in the will of God, for they are God's will realizing itself through us. And their first condition is that they must be according to God's will. Prayers may indeed, and often do, change what *appears* to be God's will—in what is His will for a time or a preliminary to something higher. Their real power exists in their being according to God's will, because God works out His will as much through our prayers as our works. This question has often caused much difficulty: How can I know that my prayers are according to the will of God? The question strikes at the very root of our prayer life, as well as our life in the will of God. It is not easy to give a conclusive answer. And yet it may be possible to give suggestions that will enable thoughtful Christians to find the answer that meets their own need. The Holy Spirit, who is to reveal the will of God and help us in prayer, must be our Teacher.

Let us, first of all, make sure that we understand the words, *"according to his will,"* correctly. Many connect the words *any thing* with this phrase and emphasize *any thing,* rather than *"according to his will."* The thing asked must be according to His will. But there is something more important than this—not only the thing asked for, but also the disposition and character of the asker must be according to God's will. Here lies the real secret of power in prayer. Two Christians both ask for something according to the will of God. He gives it to one and not to another. And why? Because the asking of the one was different from the other. We must connect the words, *"according to His will,"* with asking. Both the thing asked and the spirit of the asking must be in harmony with God's will.

The primary importance of the latter is evident from our Lord's teaching to His disciples. He continually connected the answer to prayer with their state when praying. They must forgive, be merciful, be humble, and believing. They must ask in His name, abide in Him in keeping His commandments, and His words must abide in them. Their lives must be according to God's will. If they would love Him and keep His commandments, He would pray to the Father for them. (See, for example, John 14:10–16.)

Only the man whose life, conduct, heart, and disposition are according to God's will can ask according to His will. So James spoke of the fervent, effectual prayer of the righteous man. (See James 5:16.) And John said, *"What-soever we ask, we receive of Him, because we keep His commandments"* (1 John 3:22). It is the life that prays. The prayer has power according to the life, and a life according to God's will can ask according to God's will.

One great reason for this is that the man who lives according to God's will is spiritually able to discern what he may ask for. A Christian may take some promise of God's Word, say, for the conversion of sinners and begin to pray for someone in the mere power of human love. He does so without seeking to be led by the Spirit into the faith that enables him to pray successfully. It is simply a matter of human will; I would like the conversion of this friend. God wills that all should be saved; I will ask it. But there is no thought of that abiding in Christ through obedience to which the promise of an answer has been given. This is not asking according to the will of God. The prayer was not offered in the deep consciousness of dependence on the Holy Spirit, nor in that true, obedient abiding in Christ Jesus, which alone is truly asking in His name.

Doing is the only way to knowing the will of God, and therefore, it is the only way of asking according to His will. As long as I desire only to know God's will with regard to certain things I desire or need, I may find it difficult to know it. A life yielded to and molded by the will of God will know what and how to pray. A heart seeking to be *filled with the knowledge of his will in all wisdom and spiritual understanding"* (Colossians 1:9) and striving fervently *"to stand perfect and complete in all the will of God"* (Colossians 4:12) will be able to joyfully appropriate the promise, *"This is the confidence that we have in him, that, if we ask any thing according to his will, he heareth us"* (1 John 5:4).

Let us try to learn the lessons. Confidence in prayer comes from the assurance that both the spirit of the asking and the thing we ask are according to the will of God. In all our prayers that we have learned from His Word, let us take time to realize that they are indeed according to God's loving, mighty will, and therefore sure to be heard. Let us remember how essentially one our lives and our prayers are, and live wholly to God's will—that shall ensure our praying according to His will. Let us first pray and wait for the things that God has clearly revealed to be His will, things that concern His love and kingdom and glory—that shall give us liberty with the lesser things that concern us.

Only the Holy Spirit in the spirit of prayer can lead us into the will of God—as we wait on Him even in the things we know to be according to God's will. He can give us divine assurance in regard to things that no human reason could believe beforehand to be God's will. Let our first desire in regard to every petition always be: Lord, teach me how to pray only according to Your will.

God's will is at first a deep, hidden mystery. He who lives to that will, as far as he knows it, may count on being led deeper into it as the manifestation of a holy, mighty, infinite goodness. Let me give myself to it as to infinite love. God works out His will equally by the works and the prayers of His people. Yield yourself equally without reserve to that will, in working as in praying, and in praying as in working. The absolute, joyful surrender of our lives to that will, in full obedience and in perfect truth, gives confidence in doing and in asking. And this text, instead of being a stumbling block, will give us new joy and confidence in prayer, because the prayer according to the will of God must prevail.

Chapter 31
The Glory of God's Will

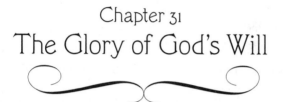

"The four and twenty elders fall down before him that sat on the throne, and worship him that liveth for ever and ever, and cast their crowns before the throne, saying, Thou art worthy, O Lord, to receive glory and honour and power: for thou hast created all things, and for thy pleasure they are and were created."
—Revelation 4:10–11

I n chapter four of the book of Revelation, we have the glory of God as Creator. The living creatures who are in the midst of the throne and around the throne have no rest, day or night, as they sing, *"Holy, holy, holy, Lord God Almighty, which was, and is, and is to come"* (verse 8). As they show forth the glory of the divine Person as Him who lives forever and ever, the four and twenty elders fall down and worship Him in His works, cast their crowns before the throne, and cry out, *"Thou art worthy, O Lord, to receive glory and honor...for thou hast created all things, and for thy pleasure they are and were created."*

In chapter five, we have the glory of God as Redeemer, where the song of the ransomed, *"Thou art worthy,"* and of the angel hosts, *"Worthy is the Lamb"* (verse 12), is followed by the adoration of all creatures, *"Blessing, and honour, and glory, and power, be unto him that sitteth upon the throne, and unto the Lamb for ever and ever"* (verse 13). In between the worship of God in the glory of His divine Being as the Thrice Holy and Everliving One and His glory of redemption with the Lamb in the midst of the throne comes the glory of His divine will as the Creator of all.

"Thou art worthy, O Lord, to receive the glory...for thou hast created all things, and for thy pleasure they are and were created." Our study of the will of God would be incomplete if we did not learn the place its worship has in heaven and, from that, the place its worship ought to have in our hearts.

In heaven, where all veils are taken away, where everything is seen in the light of God, and God is known, the elders, at the thought that God has been pleased to will creation into existence, fall down on their faces in worship.

The Glory of God's Will

They cast their crowns before the throne and give Him glory because of His will. God's glory shines out in His works. The connecting link between the glory of His divine Person and of the works He has made is His will. This is the highest glory of creation—that the God of all glory has willed it. It is the expression and embodiment of His all-perfect and almighty will and so bears the stamp of His divine glory.

The glory of the Creator and the glory of mankind are united in the glory of the divine will, the connecting link between the two. In heaven, creation is seen to be nothing but the manifestation of the presence, power, and goodness of God in every detail. And the heavenly beings are seen as the mouthpieces and interpreters of creation—they do not cease to give glory to this all-creating will. And it is because they see the glory of God's will and adore it that they delight in doing it as it is done in heaven.

If we are to do God's will on earth as it is done in heaven, we need the same spirit of adoration and worship. Each of us needs to have our heart opened to the inconceivably wondrous thought, "Because of God's will, I have and am what I am. God has willed me into existence. That will maintains me every moment. In virtue of that will, I am His redeemed child. I can count on that will to carry out its purpose and effect its object in me. Here I am, the workmanship of the glorious will of the Thrice Holy and Ever-living God. I am His handiwork, partaking of and manifesting His glory. Every moment of my existence, every power of my being, may be the embodiment, the manifestation of God's will."

Surely if our eyes and hearts are opened to see this, we would also fall prostrate and worship. *"Thou art worthy...to receive glory... for thy pleasure they are and were created."* And if we as yet have no crowns to cast before the throne, each of us has that which is as the crown of his being—his will, his heart, his life, his love—to offer to Him who sits upon the throne. Continually say, "You are worthy to receive the glory, whose will has made us the objects of Your creating and redeeming love."

God created us to show forth the glory of His will. This thought, at the close of our meditations, gives new urgency to the call to live to the will of God. You remember how, in our opening chapter, we saw what the four great aspects are under which God's will is revealed to us. In regard to each of these, this adoring acknowledgement that we owe our being to God's will enables us all the better to give His will the place and the honor to which it has a claim.

The Glory of God's Will

There is God's will in *providence. As* I worship the will that brought me forth, that never
ceases its work in me, and that connects every
trial that comes to me, I will be enabled to
rejoice even in tribulation. I will be able to
bear all as part of the blessed will of the One
whose I am and whom I serve.

There is God's will in His *precepts.* As I
see how these originate in the will of His creating love and are the guides to the cooperation with Him that will ensure His perfecting
His work in me, my whole heart welcomes
His every command. I offer prostrate worship to give glory to Him who sits on the
throne.

There is God's will in His *promises.* These
too, acquire new preciousness, certainty, and
power. We have the assurance of faith in the
will that created and upholds all cares, in the
minutest detail, for our weakness and need.
It provides sufficient grace for a perfect corre-
spondence on our part to what it is working in
us.

And, then, there is God's will in His eternal, worldwide *purpose.* The vision of the will
that embraces all creation has made me part
of it. It has made His own glory dependent on
its and my own destiny. It enlarges my heart
to feel that my true and only glory is to yield
myself as a willing instrument to its service

and to live only so that His will may triumph throughout the whole earth.

Oh, the glory of the will of God! In Him who sits upon the throne! In the universe that He created to show forth that will! In the heavenly hosts who worship before the throne, where that will is enthroned in glory! In the Beloved Son, who came as man to do that will on earth! In the heart of the believer, who has yielded his life to be conformed to it! In the church, through which that will is working out its eternal purpose in the world! Oh, the glory of the will of God! Let us gaze, worship, and give glory to God until the will of God rules the thrones of our hearts as it does the throne of heaven, and until it is done in our life *"on earth, as it is in heaven"* (Matthew 6:10).

Lord Jesus, who taught us to pray *"Thy will be done in earth, as it is in heaven"* (verse 10), we look to You. Oh, teach us to live thus!

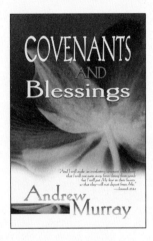